CW01303867

Also by J.W. Tapper

Humberside CID
Book One: Cold Inside
Book Two: Old Scars

Blood:Lust
Book One: Midnight Cocktail
Book Two: Cheating Sunrise

The Truth About Kate Hayes
Part One: Kissing The Scorpion
Part Two: Playing The Ace
Part Three: Painting The Dragon

ARCADE LIFE

Life versus Video Games
A personal account of Left-Right-Fire
and everything that followed

J.W. Tapper

Copyright © 2020 by J.W. Tapper

All rights reserved. No part of this publication may be reproduced, distributed, or transmitted in any form or by any means, including photocopying, recording, or other electronic or mechanical methods, without the prior written permission of the author, except in the case of brief quotations in critical reviews and certain other non-commercial uses permitted by copyright law.

This is a work of non-fiction. Characters, businesses, places, events and incidents are real, and described as factually as I remember them. Where a real person is mentioned in relation to an activity which is in any way illegal, embarrassing or just plain stupid, I have changed their name out of consideration and to avoid getting sued, punched or both.

If you were there, and you don't remember this stuff the way I remember it, that's my fault entirely.

Formatting
Polgarus Studio - www.polgarusstudio.com

This one is for Ben Locke.

Honourable mentions (in absolutely no particular order) to: Quantum Sheep, Martin Giaco, Jeff Minter, Keith Otto, Stephen Danton, Sadboy, Johnny Butt, Rob, Andy, Grant, Smiley, Nikolai Ostertag, Bob Drake, Cliff Hall, Joel Collins, Ade Wilson, Silky, Carl, Kev, Paul Martin, Helen Maddocks, Anthony Mabee, Bruno BlindDog Smith, John Willicombe, a bloke called Trevor who I never met in real life, The Jesters of Middle Earth from LotRO, and Dean Ryan.

Thanks to everyone who designed, developed, or was otherwise involved with creating the arcade games of the late seventies and early eighties. That's where it all started.

You want to play at war
But you don't like it when I shoot back

Dum - 'Something'

Chapter 0
Attract mode
'What's the most important thing in life?'

There's a generic personality survey question that regularly shows up in lifestyle magazines and during interviews with generic personality pop stars. The question asks 'Which of the following is the most important thing in life?' and the respondent must choose one answer from these three options: money, friendship or health. When I was creating the website for my second band, Dum, I made up a list of mostly stupid questions for each band member to answer so we could have a 'find out about the band' page on the website. One of the stupid questions I used was the bog-standard 'money, friendship, health' survey question. When I answered that question, I chose 'health', then I added a comment beneath my answer: 'Actually, video games are more important'.

That was in early 2001, when I was thirty-seven years old, ten years before Skyrim was released on 11/11/11 and more than twenty years since I first played Space Invaders in my local village pub. That moment in 2001 isn't particularly relevant, but my response to that question still haunts me now, near the end of 2019, raising its mocking middle finger at me across the gulf of years against a backdrop of mundane real-world memories linked inexorably to far more vivid recollections of Asteroids, Doom, Mr Do's Castle, R-Type, Tomb Raider, Gauntlet, Bombjack, Morrowind, Donkey Kong, Galaga, Altered Beast, Diablo II, Frogger, Deus Ex, Joust, Pac-Man, Smash TV, Space Invaders…

Like all autobiographies, or at least like the ones I've idly flicked through in Tesco when I should have been buying milk and bananas, this one is going to start right back at the beginning.

Chapter 1

Going to The Moon
'Do that thing where you shoot the big one last.'

I was born in 1963, in Birmingham, England, a couple of weeks before JFK was assassinated, a convenient time to be born for someone who was going to be getting hooked on arcade games at an appropriate age. Not that I'm saying any kind of addiction is a good thing, just that I was the right age at the right time, as far as getting access to video games in the very early eighties was concerned.

By 1969 my family had moved from Birmingham to a small village called Tarrington in Herefordshire. We lived in the school house because my father was head of the local primary school and it was common to get the house thrown in as part of the Headmaster deal back then. Might still be the way it is now for all I know, but I kind of doubt it. One of the few things I remember from that period, or at least I'm aware it happened, was watching the Apollo 11 moon landing from inside a den I'd built out of sofa cushions in our front room. One of the other things I remember was jumping out of a tree onto the roof of a large outbuilding in next door's garden and crashing through the rotten wood to land in a rather spectacularly lucky heap between two ancient, rusting, metal farming contraptions. Could have died right there and then at the grand old age of seven, but didn't. My father wasn't impressed. He had to pay to get their shed roof fixed.

When we moved into that school house we inherited a black cat called Smokey who had been living there with the previous Head's family and decided to stay. Or maybe they'd just left her behind due to her propensity for getting knocked up and pumping out half a dozen kittens every few months. She was a good mother, she used to cripple mice and sit quietly watching as her kittens tore them to pieces in our back yard. As a child, I found it all quite fascinating. A good introduction to nature, survival and the indifferent brutality of cats.

By the time I started at grammar school in September 1974, we had moved from Tarrington to Garway, another small village in Herefordshire, a few miles from the Welsh border. Once again, the school house was part of the local headship deal and we didn't move out of it until a few years later, when my father got a job at a bigger school, at which point we moved barely a hundred yards up the road into a new bungalow.

I have hardly any good memories of grammar school until I entered the sixth form, which I was obliged to do as I wasn't legally old enough to leave school at the end of the fifth form. The reason for that was having been put through the eleven-plus examination a year early at the age of ten, supposedly to see how well I would do, passing the test and being told I was going to grammar school a year early, and always being a year ahead of the school year where I should have been. Looking back, I don't think the early start at grammar school was such a great idea and I am fairly sure it didn't add anything positive to my time there. I was the second youngest in my year, just one day older than the youngest kid, with children older than me in the year below mine, and I finished my fifth year of secondary education in the summer of 1979 when I was still fifteen.

The sixth form was great. All the annoying, dickhead bullies who had plagued the previous five years were gone, off to shovel shit on daddy's farm and have horrifying drunken motorcycle accidents by all accounts. Damn shame. Those of us who stayed on for the sixth form were now officially being treated as young adults instead of children by the teaching staff. The strategy didn't work with me because I was still very much a stupid kid, a phase that lasted for at least another...what day is it now? Anyway, we had our own sixth-form study room, which I hardly ever used, and our own sixth-form common room full of recreational activities, which I hardly ever left. The common room was a large, open-plan first-floor area with a kitchen, cheaply upholstered seating along the walls, table tennis, a record player with your actual stereo speakers, a dartboard and a pool table. If I had to cite one specific reason why I flunked my A-levels the first time I took them, it would have to be that pool table.

I played darts and pool before I encountered video games.

I quite liked darts, but I absolutely loved playing pool. I wasn't even that good at it but that didn't stop me playing it as often as possible, watching other people play when it wasn't my turn on the table. Apart from wrecking my A levels, playing pool inevitably led me to the local village pub, The Garway Moon, and that was also the place where I would have my first experience with a video game – the beginning of the end, if you like.

I started going to the pub in 1980 to play pool, darts, and music on the jukebox. The Moon was a typical country village pub: small, low-ceilinged, painted black and white on the outside, and usually half full of serious-looking farmers and other species of real working men on the inside. We used to say it had no atmosphere, because it was The Moon, and the joke was funnier because we knew it was just a feeble, predictable pun, funnier still because it so accurately described the inhospitable ambience generated by the landlady and her regular clientele.

My friends and I weren't quite old enough to legally be sold anything alcoholic but we could go in the pub, buy an orange juice, and get some change for the pool table without annoying too many of the regulars in the bar. The pool table, darts and jukebox were in a separate room from the public bar, a familiar setup to that of many pubs back then. The old games room at the Garway Moon is a restaurant now, which is the same way that most village pubs have gone. Either that or they've been converted into flats or residential homes for the elderly, or simply knocked down to make room for an entire Legoland-looking housing estate.

Being a quiet village pub, they tended not to have anything particularly rowdy on the jukebox. No punk rock or heavy metal, that's for sure. The noisiest band on there was Queen. We used to continually play 'Crazy Little Thing Called Love' and, more frequently, the B-side, a live version of 'We Will Rock You'. That was the best thing on that jukebox for ages, and we tried our hardest to wear it out.

The pool table was prone to giving out free games, particularly if you covertly jammed a matchstick under the coin slider when it was just far enough out to keep the ball return chute stuck in place so the balls could be continually retrieved at the end of the table. So, on top of selling us just the one orange juice a night, they weren't exactly making a fortune out of our pool-playing habits either. The dartboard was legitimately free and usually monopolised by a crowd of Young Farmers, another great reason for me to stay well away from it. I would have enjoyed playing darts in the pub if I could do mental subtraction a hell of a lot better than I can. It's embarrassing, standing there failing dismally to take treble nineteen away from 301, when you know half the farmers in the pub could do it without blinking. I didn't play darts very often in the pub, unless I could convince someone else to do the scoring.

Not long after I started going to the Garway Moon they installed a Space Invaders cabinet in the games room, shoved into a corner to the right of the jukebox, near the doorway into the bar. I can remember it perfectly, particularly the rather large red buttons, and it will forever be *my first video game*. I immediately became obsessed with it. I stopped taking my turn on the pool table and I no longer had many spare 10p coins for the jukebox. Darts, always a mere standby for me, was now completely ignored.

I wasn't the only person who played that particular Space Invaders machine, but I was easily the one who was most hooked, spending more time on it than anyone else. I played it so much that I didn't have to think about what I was doing. I'm sure, if you have played any of those early video games to the extent that I did, you will know exactly what I mean. The pulse of the game, the heartbeat, gets so far inside your own head that following the game's simple rhythms becomes completely instinctive.

Most of the people who played Space Invaders in The Moon were young blokes. I hardly ever saw girls playing on it, but I do remember them playing darts and pool. One of the local girls who didn't play Space Invaders was a tall blonde called Rebecca. I had reached the point where I was so familiar with the timing mechanics of Space Invaders that I could let someone else press the fire button while I operated the left/right buttons and still consistently get scores over five thousand. This rudimentary simultaneous two-player mode was achieved by having the other person stand right next to me, making actual physical contact, for as long as the game lasted. I could make a game of Space Invaders last a heck of a long time, especially with a girl who didn't play Space Invaders pressing the fire button in a random rhythm totally lacking in syncopation but entirely compensated by that necessary close physical proximity.

Rebecca was too cool to hang out with a gamer on anything more than an infrequent, temporary basis, although nobody was being called a gamer back then, but she tolerated the tedium of pressing the fire button for me on more than one occasion and she even took a ride on the big wheel at Barry Island with me, which was recklessly flirting with rusty, creaking metallic death but still qualified as a fun day out.

Almost without exception, everyone else I saw playing Space Invaders in the pub was perfectly happy having one go before wandering off to play pool or to buy another drink and stand around chatting about the latest sheep-shearing contest. I couldn't understand how they could do that. Not the sheep-shearing, that made some sort of *sense* because I lived in an area where farming-related activities were the norm. No, it was the way most people could just blithely dip their toe into the Space Invaders experience and casually pull it out again without seeming to care when they were going to have another go. I couldn't do that. Couldn't just have one go and walk away, at least not until I was capable of making that 'one go' last more than two hours.

Right from the start, when each game was barely lasting a minute, I instinctively knew I wanted to keep playing, repeatedly ramming 10p coins into the slot and jabbing the Player One button, constantly progressing further and further through the endless screens of lumbering monochrome aliens. I was driven to achieve a high score, then a higher score, and then the highest score possible, which was 9990 on Space Invaders because it only had a four-digit high-score counter.

At this point it would be fairly obvious, even to me, to point smugly at that dark little corner of the past and say, "You were addicted to that game." I most certainly was, but nobody was thinking about video game addiction in 1980, at least they weren't thinking about it in small village pubs. That's not to say that my obsession didn't have its problems.

First of all, the opening hours for public houses in the early eighties were a lot shorter than they are now. I used to regularly walk a quarter of a mile from our house to the pub on a Sunday and wait outside on my own for it to open at midday. I'd go in, put 10p in the Space Invaders machine (with no longer even the pretence of buying a token orange juice) and play until the pub shut at 2 p.m., then I'd walk home and eat a very late Sunday lunch. Towards the end of my time with that Space Invaders machine, those two hours would be one single game and I'd still have a couple of lives left when the pub shut and it was time to go.

One of the many lessons life taught me via video games was that being good at Space Invaders in a village pub was sometimes more trouble than it was worth. As I mentioned earlier, the highest score that could be achieved was 9990, after which the score clocked back to zero because it couldn't display anything higher. Once I had mastered the two key techniques for achieving Space Invaders high scores – counting shots and the Wall-of-Death (aka Death Row) – I was regularly clocking the high-score multiple times in a game, deliberately losing my remaining lives to leave an eventual high score of 9990. This tended to annoy some people, particularly the Young Farmers and other casual Space Invaders players who thought earning the extra life (at 1500 points) was an impressive feat. On one occasion, after passing various unsubtle comments such as "I wonder if he plays as well with a boot up the arse?" and seeing that I was completely ignoring them, a group of rather peeved Young Farmers (who were all a few years older than me, but still getting their jollies at sheep-shearing competitions and ploughing matches) asked me to stop setting a high-score of 9990 because how were they ever supposed to get the high score if I always left 9990 on there? Of course, I had to do as they asked because they were so polite and well-spoken… so I started leaving the high-score as 9980 instead. Call me juvenile, selfish, silly and arrogant if you like. I certainly was.

Those two techniques – counting shots and the Wall-of-Death – had been shown to me by someone who was just passing through Garway and had stopped at the pub for a pint and a quick game of Space Invaders. I didn't know them but I watched them play for a while, and I started up a conversation because I could see they knew more about the game than I did. Constantly getting the maximum 300 points when shooting the supposedly random-scoring mystery ship was a bit of a giveaway.

Once you were good enough to get through the phase where the first screen was a panicky mess, and you were able to regularly clear three or four screens, it was time to start counting your shots. The supposedly random mystery ship's value actually cycled through a fixed score pattern depending on the number of shots fired by the player. The most popular way of exploiting this was to fire twenty-two shots at the start of a screen, hit the ship for 300 points, then hit it with every fifteenth shot, for 300 points each time, until the end of the screen, restarting the counting on each subsequent screen with twenty-two shots. If you have the original Space Invaders ROM for MAME (Multiple Arcade Machine Emulator - more about that later) you can try that method of shot counting for yourself.

The Wall of Death, alternatively referred to as Death Row, involved exploiting the fact that, on the very last row before a game-ending invasion, the invaders' shots don't destroy the player's gun. The trick was to set up a block of five columns of invaders (usually the five columns on the right) with a cleared two-column gap and then a single top-row invader to the left. After that, you kept your laser mostly in the safe zone of the two clear columns, so you could continue to count shots and snipe the 300-point mystery ships while waiting for the five-column block of invaders to reach 'death row' where they couldn't kill you. The only tricky part came when you had to shoot the final row of five invaders and then hit the last one after the two-column gap. If your timing was off and you missed him, he would drop down into the 'invasion' row and it would be instant Game Over, no matter how many lives you had left. 'Game Over' are the two worst words in the world, by the way.

Another trick, that wouldn't have any scoring benefit until Space Invaders Part II, but which occasionally impressed my small audience in the pub, was to shoot all the invaders apart from one whole column and then destroy that column from the top down, leaving one of the large ten-point invaders until the end. Doing this would cause the last invader to draw a glitchy white fence behind him as he raced back and forth across the screen.

From memory, which is really all I have to go on for the early eighties, the best score I managed to achieve in one of my two-hour single-game Sunday lunchtime sessions was just over 72,000 points – clocking the game past 9990 seven times – which involved clearing over thirty screens. In theory, once you were able to clear the tenth screen, you could play indefinitely because the game reset back to the difficulty of the first screen after every tenth screen was cleared, so the only thing limiting my high-score potential was the opening hours of the pub. It's quite hard to comprehend this now, even though I lived through it, when comparing it to the availability and portability of an almost infinite number of different video games these days. For a while, the only way I could play a video game was by walking to the village pub, and that was just on Friday and Saturday evenings, and lunch time on Sunday.

The only other significant memory I have of that Space Invaders machine in the Garway Moon was being shown how to get free credits by holding down a combination of the control buttons and the player selection buttons during a specific sequence of the game's attract mode. The most surprising thing about this trick was that it worked every time, and not just on that particular machine.

That's not an urban myth, it's not 'something that happened to a friend of a friend', I was shown how to do it and I absolutely assure you it worked. All I can think is that it was a secret backdoor feature added by one of the Taito nerds who either forgot to remove it or left it in to surprise and delight future generations.

The landlady at The Moon must have eventually figured out what was happening, probably because someone showed off their expert Invaders free-game knowledge to the wrong person, or she noticed the machine was no longer making much money despite always being in use.

One Sunday, while I was there playing Space Invaders on my own, a couple of jovial, long-haired Arcade Game Fixer Blokes turned up and proceeded to interrupt my game. They asked me rather rhetorically how much fun I was having playing for free, and I believe I did a fair impersonation of someone who has not a clue about what is being spoken. Without even bothering to disconnect the power they took the front off the machine, passing various sarcastic comments in my direction while fiddling about inside the cabinet. Promising me that my days of free credits were now over, they closed the cabinet and sauntered off into the bar to celebrate their victory with a couple of pints of presumably piss-weak draught beer.

Ironically, I always paid for the games when I went to the pub on my own. I was getting a full two-hours entertainment for only 10p and I suspected that a completely empty coin box would arouse suspicion, with me the fairly obvious suspect as I was the only person playing for the whole time. On that Sunday, however, I waited until Botch Cassidy and Somedunce Kid were fully immersed in drinking their pints before quickly trying the free credits trick. It still worked, which felt like a major victory to me, and I took great personal delight smiling and saluting them around the doorframe as they sat at the bar and I enjoyed a free game on the 'fixed' machine.

Not long after that, early in 1981, presumably more through desperation at lost profits than because the landlady wanted to give her thieving underage customers a shiny new video game to play on, Space Invaders was replaced by another game from Taito: Lunar Rescue. I believe they just swapped some of the circuit boards out, as the cabinet and buttons weren't changed.

Replacing Space Invaders with Lunar Rescue at my local pub meant I no longer had easy access to Space Invaders. That was a crushing blow, a major test of my character, willpower and agility. Well, no, not my agility. That was just a bit of a foreshadowing joke for anyone reading this who might be wondering if I'll ever get to the part where I burned thousands of hours on computer role-playing games. Be patient, your time will come.

Lunar Rescue was my difficult second video game, the

same way that some bands have difficult second albums. It also started off being literally my difficult second video game.

Space Invaders was a straightforward fixed shooter, although the term 'fixed shooter' had not yet been coined in the Garway Moon because the only video game we'd ever seen was Space Invaders. Lunar Rescue, despite sharing the Space Invaders cabinet and hardware, had multiple game elements, horizontal and vertical ship movement, two distinctly different game phases, and basic non-aggressive objectives involving rescuing people from the planet's surface and taking them back to the hovering mothership.

It also let you personalise your high score with ten alphanumeric characters of your choice. They must have had a couple of very naive nerds working on Lunar Rescue at Taito, because what's the average teenage kid likely to do when offered ten free-text characters to display a message for all to see? Sorry to disappoint, but I mostly put the names of my favourite bands on there, making as much use of the maximum ten characters as possible, so maybe the Taito nerds were not so naive but were also fans of bands with ten-character names such as Stranglers and The Damned.

I applied the same level of relentless dedication to mastering Lunar Rescue that I'd used on Space Invaders. Left-right-fire was still the foundation of the player's interaction with the on-screen action but Lunar Rescue introduced additional elements such as vertical player movement, the concept of accurate landing, and fuel-management during the descent phase. It was a mind-blowing step up from Space

Invaders and it heralded the first instance of what was going to become a standard question from eager-yet-baffled new players of many subsequent video games, where the objective was not to simply shoot everything in sight: "What do you have to do?"

On my father's fifty-first birthday in the summer of 1981 I almost killed myself by drinking heroically stupid amounts of wine and spirits in the kitchen of our bungalow. I'm not proud of it but it was funny at the time, although not for me. I spent an hour lying outside the back door on a concrete path, physically unable to move, with my head over a drain, and I was ill for the following three days. I had invited a few of my friends over and they managed to get me out of the house while I was still capable of walking, before the head-over-the-drain episode.

They took me up the road to the pub and stood me in front of Lunar Rescue. Although I was completely paralytic, I got the high score and set the ten characters to HIIIIIIIII before staggering out of the pub and attempting to climb onto the roof of a nearby bus shelter. After falling off the side of the bus shelter, I announced that I felt fine before projectile vomiting all over the road.

My friend Rob walked me back home, encouraging me to "Think of the [UK] Subs" and spit, which he sincerely believed would help me cope with the onset of severe alcohol poisoning. Days later, I found out he had been chasing my other friends around the bungalow with my air rifle, shooting them with felt cleaning pellets. There's not much more I remember about that night. I was woken up the next morning by my father, who found my appalling hangover quite amusing until he noticed the hole I'd punched through my bedroom door.

Lunar Rescue was an interesting development after Space Invaders, bringing new concepts such as dodging horizontally scrolling spaceships and meteors, and rescuing people, but it wasn't a huge change of pace from the earlier Taito game.

Although I didn't know it, something truly revolutionary was heading my way, a life-affirming experience of pure bliss you're only otherwise going to hear about from a compulsive liar or a terminal drug addict. It was the next game they installed in The Moon, the final arcade game I played in that pub before being formally banned. I still consider it to be one of the greatest arcade games ever made, and its arrival marked a point in time where video games began to fill more and more hours of my life, influencing larger decisions and changing the way I dealt with the real world. That game was Asteroids.

Chapter 2

Memories of The Golden Age
'Coin detected in pocket.'

In the early eighties, video games were a novelty but they weren't just some trivial fad. They were huge. Brand new, fresh over from Japan or the USA, everybody wanted to play them and talk about them. You couldn't go in a pub, café, Fish and Chip shop or Chinese takeaway without seeing a small crowd of people – mostly teenage boys – hunched around an arcade cabinet, with those waiting for their go lining up 10p coins along the bottom of the screen and forming an enthusiastic crowd of supporters and hecklers for this bizarre new spectator sport.

I had served a covert apprenticeship on Space Invaders and Lunar Rescue, hidden away in a secluded village pub while I honed my left-right-fire skills and attained a certain level of mastery on those primitive games. That comfortable seclusion changed rapidly, and the number of video games vying for my time exploded exponentially.

Much like an ever-expanding map of unlocked waypoints in an open-world RPG, the number of gaming locations in my life grew steadily throughout the early eighties. The village pub stayed relevant for a while, a low-level noob base I was reluctant to abandon even when I'd levelled up beyond its limited resources. To encourage me to fly the nest they banned me, presumably after I reached the required number of complaints from all the real drinking men who couldn't beat my scores on Space Invaders and Asteroids.

Attending the sixth form in Ross-on-Wye gave me a weekday hub for lunchtime gaming sessions at a variety of venues ranging from the fairly safe Fred's Café (notable games: Pac-Man, Space Invaders Part II) to the genuinely scary Barrel pub (notable game: Galaxian) and the small arcade on the ground floor of Jaqueline's nightclub that was open during the day for reasons most likely related to maximising profit (notable games: Battlezone, Moon Cresta, Defender, Berzerk).

There were other pubs within a rough ten-mile radius of where I lived. The Fountain Inn at Orcop had a tabletop Space Invaders, where I tested the free credits trick and proved it worked on machines other than the one in The Moon. The game I remember most at The Duke of Wellington, a pub on a narrow B-road to Monmouth, was Crazy Climber, a bizarre dual-stick tabletop machine where the player character's arms were moved independently via separate joysticks. The New Inn at St. Owen's Cross had Iron Horse followed by Green Beret, and The Harewood End Inn on the main Ross-Hereford road had Qix followed by Amidar.

In Monmouth there was a little independent record shop called Round Ear Records, run by a post-hippy-era bloke with the fabulous name John Willicombe, with a whole mini-arcade of constantly changing machines. That was the first place I ever played Frogger and Donkey Kong. They also had Missile Command, Robotron 2084 and Asteroids.

Asteroids had an immediate, life-changing effect on me. If Space Invaders was the tempting harlot who first got me hooked on video games, Asteroids was the crack-pushing pimp in a massive stretch Cadillac, gleefully leeching a constant, jingling haemorrhage of 10p coins from me in exchange for the ultimate video gaming high: a ridiculously fast, free-moving, triangular ship firing glowing shots of white light while navigating a perilous barrage of spinning vector-graphic rocks that shattered in the empty black void of space.

Asteroids was arcade gaming purity. It was as close to perfect as any game would ever be. It was brilliant, as simple or complex as the player could imagine it to be. And, at first, it was insanely hard.

After the simple, evolutionary step between Space Invaders and Lunar Rescue, the radical new concepts introduced by Asteroids were a jarring challenge. The challenge was too much for some people, storming away from the machine in a rage after ten seconds of yelling impotently at the little triangular ship while it lurched and spun out of control into the nearest rock tumbling slowly across the screen. I saw the same reaction five years later when I was taking an entrance test to be a computer programmer with the Civil Service. We were handed a question sheet with something like a hundred complex maths problems on it, and given twenty minutes to complete the test. After what can't have been more than thirty seconds, one bloke shoved his chair back, stood up, loudly announced, "This is stupid! How do they expect us to do this?" before storming out through the door, narrowly avoiding a well-paid-but-soulless grey-suited future in an open-plan office.

Exactly the same with Asteroids, some people just didn't get it and couldn't deal with their own limitations when faced with what initially appeared to be an insurmountable challenge.

I went the other way, of course. I played and crashed and burned and died and played and spun wildly out of control and played and died and played and laughed when I died and played…and I learned. You had to learn how to play Asteroids or you never got past the second wave of rocks or the first appearance of the smaller of the two UFOs.

At first, our golden rule was "Don't use thrust! You'll die!" but we soon learned the opposite was true. "If you don't use thrust, you'll die."

In Space Invaders, learning to move the player gun left and right with the buttons or joystick was simple. Progress and high scores came from mastering a few strategies and tactics, and getting enough practice on the game that the timing of every movement and shot became totally intuitive and natural. Asteroids had left and right buttons but they didn't move the ship across the screen, they rotated it in place. The left button rotated the ship anti-clockwise, the right button rotated it clockwise. This was enough of a shock for some players, and then there was the thrust button and all its associated inertia-related challenges, the wraparound screen, and the apparent randomness of the rocks and the way they broke into smaller pieces when shot.

There was a fifth button, Hyperspace, a tempting panic-button often jabbed within the first few seconds by new players who immediately regretted the decision when the ship vanished, only to reappear directly in the path of a hurtling chunk of space debris. As last resorts go, Hyperspace put the 'catch' in Catch 22. If you needed to use it, then you weren't good enough to benefit from the extra few seconds it might grant you, and if you were good enough to benefit from using it, then you never used it. It didn't take me long to decide Hyperspace was a scapegoat button for cry-baby players. If you were nifty enough at flying the ship to dodge ninety-nine percent of your close calls, you'd crash before you even considered using Hyperspace, because on later levels you'd be less than half a second from disaster almost the whole time.

I loved everything about Asteroids. The futuristically minimalist vector graphics with their afterimage ghosting, the ominous booms of the exploding rocks, the jump-scare beeping heralding the appearance of a UFO initially causing panic but later becoming a welcome audible announcement of an imminent score boost. But more than all of that, it was the way the player controlled the ship, and the feeling of freedom and, ultimately, the illusion of invincibility the control method imparted.

Before they took the Lunar Rescue game away and replaced it with Asteroids in The Moon, I'd already seen an Asteroids machine at The Mumbles Pier arcade during a holiday to The Gower in the summer of 1980. There had been a kid playing it who was wearing a homemade Asteroids T-shirt, just a black top with the Asteroids player ship and some rocks drawn on it, looking like it had been done with a silver marker pen. I remember I watched him play for a while before deciding the game looked too hard and just too complicated to risk playing for the first time in front of a throng of gawping spectators when I knew I wouldn't last more than a handful of seconds.

There was no such trepidation when the shiny new Asteroids cabinet arrived at The Moon. I'd mastered Space Invaders and Lunar Rescue, and I was more than ready for the welcome challenge of a new game.

Getting proficient at high-speed, reckless navigation of the asteroid belt was pretty much the dictionary definition of both 'showing off' and 'really cool'. Whereas a Space Invaders high score of 9990 looked good, and reaching level ten without losing a single life impressed a few people, blasting through a chaotic late-level Asteroids screen was an unrivalled crowd-baiting spectacle of rock-busting sharpshooting and a breakneck-speed series of near misses and physics-defying bravado.

I pulled my first proper video game crowd on the Asteroids machine in Round Ear Records. Countless sessions at The Moon had got me to the point where I could repeatedly clock Asteroids past its top score of 99,990 and amass a long line of extra lives due to a new one being awarded every 10,000 points.

On a couple of occasions in The Moon, during long single-game sessions, I remember asking someone to look after my long-running game while I took a toilet break, and coming back to find that even though they'd died a dozen or so times I still had a long line of extra lives on the screen.

During a similar session in the record shop I'd clocked the score once and was halfway to doing it again, long line of extra lives on the screen, and I looked over my shoulder to see a small crowd of faces just staring at me, some looking totally in awe and others looking pissed off at having to wait so long for a go. I remember thinking I needed to do something more significant than just carrying on playing so I asked who was next on and let them take over while I casually wandered away to see what second-hand coloured-vinyl punk EPs were going cheap.

As with Space Invaders, my friends rarely wanted to play a two-player game of Asteroids with me (taking alternate turns every time a player lost a life) because I could make the first ship last longer than they were likely to make their whole game last. I'd do things like rush to the first extra life at 10,000 points and deliberately crash, just so they could have their go without waiting ages, then I'd play properly once their game had ended.

Asteroids was the first game I played where there was a high-score leaderboard. It showed the ten highest scores achieved, each with a three-character uppercase alphabetic signature. This seemed like a step backwards from the ten-character high-score signature in Lunar Rescue, but three characters became the unofficial standard for high-score signatures so we learned to work with what we were given. Back then I was mostly being called JT by my friends, and in my head it was Jay Tee because that's how my brain works, so it was obvious to me that I should sign my Asteroids high scores JAY.

I was in the sixth form at Ross-On-Wye's John Kyrle High School from September 1979 to the spring of 1982. I had to stay a few extra months to re-sit two A-level exams because I had colossally screwed them up the first time I took them in the summer of 1981. I like to blame the pool table in the common room for my A-level train-wreck but my arcade-gaming habit was not entirely blameless.

Most lunch hours I'd walk into town and spend a few 10p pieces in one of the places I mentioned earlier: Fred's Café, The Barrel pub or the ground floor arcade in Jacqueline's Nightclub.

The first time I played Space Invaders Part II was in Fred's Café on a cocktail table machine where the screen was set horizontally into the tabletop and you played the game sitting down instead of standing up at a vertical cabinet. It gave you somewhere to put your cup of tea or bottle of Cresta, and cafés could just swap a regular table for a cocktail machine instead of having to make room for a vertical cabinet.

During that first game on Space Invaders Part II, a local

know-it-all hanger-on fake-hardman (you know the type) called Skinner came up to the table and told me I wouldn't be able to do the death row trick after the third screen because of the splitters. He sounded very sure of this and did a lot of exasperated arm waving, so I told him to watch while I proceeded to execute a particularly satisfying death row on the fourth screen. Armed with the shocking news that death rows were actually possible on Space Invaders Part II, he waddled off, red-faced and gasping, to report back to whatever genuine local hardmen were currently not in prison.

The ground floor of the town's grubby nightclub was an amazing place. They had loads of games in there, subdued lighting, a lot of smoke, all part of that fabulous arcade atmosphere that came and went before we really had a chance to fully appreciate just how wonderful it was.

I first met many of the classics of the Golden Age in that place; some I instantly adored, for example Stern's Berzerk, and with others I fell into a protracted love/hate relationship. Unsurprisingly the latter group of games included Williams' Defender. One of the girls who worked in the arcade was incredibly good at Defender. I watched her play it a few times and I couldn't even figure out how she was so good because she made it look effortless, and it absolutely was not an easy game by anyone's standards. Defender was one of those games I knew I should have been able to play well, and I wanted to be good at it, but I never progressed past a level of substandard mediocrity.

Another game they had there was Atari's Battlezone, a first-person perspective sci-fi tank shoot-em-up with a two-stick control method where the tank was steered very much like a real tank. The cabinet had a periscope viewer for the player to look through, which must have seemed like a wonderful idea to someone at Atari but didn't really improve the game, or make it a good one for spectators. Battlezone was really ahead of its time, possibly a little too far ahead of its time for gamers like me in 1981 (it was released in November 1980). We weren't ready for 3D first-person shooters back then, most of us were still getting to grips with shooting things on a screen in two dimensions.

For a while, the cabinet next to Battlezone was Berzerk, a weird, minimalist maze game with evil robots. They moved slowly, or not at all, the maze walls killed you if you blundered into them, and if you took too long to finish a screen an unkillable bouncing smiley face appeared and usually killed you within a few seconds. Berzerk had digitised speech, saying things like 'Intruder detected' during a game, and also 'Coin detected in pocket' during the attract mode, the latter phrase being frequently quoted by me and my friends for many years after Berzerk itself had long gone.

There were a few other games in that nightclub arcade that were part of the first wave of the Golden Age, but none that stand out as monumental highlights for me. Two worth mentioning were Nichibutsu's Moon Cresta, with its frustrating docking sequence that interrupted an otherwise fairly decent shooter, and Tempest, a colourful, pseudo-3D vector-graphics game from Atari, which was yet another pioneer of a bizarre subgenre.

The only place I ever saw a Crazy Climber machine was a pub called The Duke of Wellington, which we always referred to as The Wellie. The pub is long gone, much like the Golden Age of video games if you want to be painfully melodramatic. Rob had a "What about my bloody principles?" episode in the car park at The Wellie when he decided he was being repressed, because we wanted him to stop pretending to sniff glue, at least while we were inside the pub, because if he didn't stop doing it we'd be asked to leave.

The Crazy Climber game was a cocktail cabinet so we could all sit around it and take the piss out of whoever was playing, another positive benefit of the tabletop format. If you've never played Crazy Climber, and I'm guessing most people haven't, it was a bonkers game with a suitably bonkers control method. The aim of the game was to climb to the top of a skyscraper while avoiding various hazards, then climb to the top of a harder building, and so on, but most of the time we barely made it to the second building. The machine had two joysticks, one controlling the climber's right hand and one controlling his left hand. You had to get an alternating up/down rhythm going on the two joysticks, pulling down on one while pushing up (to reach up to the next window ledge) on the other. If one of the joysticks was knackered, or even slightly unresponsive, the game became unplayable. Of course, due to the constant, frantic up/down hammering they received, the joystick mechanisms didn't last very long. It was a shame, because the game was pretty good, although rather hard, even with fully functional joysticks. Many of the hazards and enemies were creatively amusing, from the huge birds crapping eggs onto your head to the giant 'not King Kong for copyright reasons' ape at the top of the first skyscraper who would cheerfully punch you off the building if you didn't race past him quickly enough. Damn those unresponsive joysticks.

During my early-to-mid teens I'd quit going on Saturday morning shopping trips to Monmouth with my parents, but the irresistible lure of video games pulled me back into it. As soon as the car was parked, I'd jump out and leg it straight to Round Ear Records. For a while, there was an Asteroids cabinet in Ruby Tuesday, a hybrid clothes shop and restaurant at the top of the main street. Ruby Tuesday was so far ahead of its time, with a restaurant right there in a clothes shop. All they were missing were the three-quid cups of coffee and they could have been part of some *Back to the Future* paradox.

I sometimes went in Ruby Tuesday for an Asteroids fix, but most of the time I was in the dingy backstreet record shop. I always think of Donkey Kong and Frogger when I think of Round Ear Records, even though I also played both those games in other places. Frogger was one of the very few games where the objective was purely to survive, the player having no offensive capability, and the enemies were identifiable as creatures, vehicles and other objects from the real world.

Loads of games borrowed concepts and game mechanics from Frogger; there's a phone game called Crossy Road which is pretty much Frogger with more forgiving gameplay.

Frogger had an optional objective to collect (in a romantic sense) a colourful frog partner on a floating log, and the game also featured a lot of different ways to die, including my own personal least-favourite-ever game feature: running out of time. If that's not the laziest, cheapest, cheesiest, most apathetic way to artificially increase the difficulty of a game, I don't know what is. So many games were (and still are) unnecessarily frustrating due to time limits. There's no technical or creative ability required to add a time limit to a game, just a complete lack of imagination. Berzerk did it in a subtle way by having Evil Otto bounce onto the screen if the player lingered too long, and that's perfectly acceptable because Otto is an additional enemy threat, a different element of the challenge, and he fits the theme of the game.

A modern example of a timer done right can be seen in Spelunky, where an unkillable ghostly bad guy appears if you take far too long to complete a level. But just having a timer run down, at which point the player character dies, for no other reason than the timer ran out, is a totally cheap cop-out.

In Frogger, you could theoretically stay in one place or just blunder about in a relatively safe area for as long as you wanted to, because that was the way they programmed the game, so they stuck a time limit on it to solve the problem they created. Why didn't they just add an eagle or an owl or some other mobile hazard that could fly onto the screen after a certain amount of time and start hunting the frog? That wouldn't have been difficult, and it would have fitted perfectly with the theme of the game. But no, they stuck a time limit on it because that was the easiest option. That's my opinion now, after close to forty years of being annoyed by time limits in video games. That's not what I was thinking when I was playing Frogger in 1981; back then, I was thinking Frogger was a brilliant game, and it really was.

Nintendo's 1981 game Donkey Kong had a timer that primarily affected the bonus score for each level, the amount of bonus points gradually reducing while you ran around on platforms, climbed ladders, jumped over barrels and whacked enemies with a collectable power-up hammer. Okay, now read that short list of game features again and consider how much of a massive influence Donkey Kong was, and how many thousands of games were spawned directly or indirectly from one or more of those fundamental gaming concepts. The entire platform game genre and all its subgenres, for example. Yes, I know about Space Panic coming out the year before Donkey Kong; I played it in an arcade at Barry Island a million years ago and I am familiar with the platforms and ladders in that game. I don't think it had anywhere near the amount of influence Donkey Kong had, although I do think it was a platform game even if the protagonist character was unable to jump. The rules governing whether or not a game ticks enough boxes to be called a platform game were still many years away from being defined online by po-faced killjoys. Space Panic had platforms and ladders, so it was a platform game. Trust me, you'd have more fun arguing about whether or not The Stranglers were a punk band.

Space Panic also had a timer, so it was an Annoying Bloody Timer game. I guess nobody wanted to define that particular genre so it was left to me to do it. You're welcome.

Despite having an absolute fixation on platform games later in my gaming life, I wasn't instantly attracted to Donkey Kong. There was a randomness to the way the barrels chose which ladders to fall down that was extremely disconcerting, until I found out about the trick where the barrel wouldn't fall down on the blocky player character if his hand was on the top rung of the ladder. Don't sue me if you try that and it doesn't work for you.

Donkey Kong was a prime example of a "What do you have to do?" game. Unless you'd played Space Panic, which was highly unlikely, this would have been your no-punches-pulled introduction to platforms and ladders in a video game.

The first few times I played Donkey Kong, I didn't get further than the second ladder because the whole game was an overload of unfamiliar concepts. Timing had always been an integral part of mastering any video game, but Donkey Kong required consistent, precisely timed movements and actions while under pressure, right from the start. Unlike the shoot-em-ups I'd conquered, it wasn't a case of figuring out the basics and then working on improving your timing; you had to get the timing right on every jump, every dash between ladders, every time, or you failed and died. Every time.

The hammer power-up was the blueprint for every risk-versus-reward power-up that followed. Collect it, and you could hit enemies and kill them for the limited amount of time it was active. But you couldn't jump or climb ladders while the hammer was active, and you couldn't drop it. And, of course, you had to time your attacks with the automatic down-swing of the hammer. Get the attack timing wrong and you'd miss the enemy, or the rolling barrel, and then die when it ran into you. I treated the hammer, at least on the first screen, as a hazard to be avoided; it was more of a liability than a power-up, and I could finish the screen quicker if I didn't collect it, which meant the screen bonus would be higher than if I'd picked up the hammer and blundered about at the bottom of the screen waiting for it to wear off.

Before Donkey Kong, most video games had one screen layout and they increased in difficulty by adding extra instances of the same hazard (example: the rocks in Asteroids) or by increasing the speed and power of enemies without changing their appearance (example: most early shoot-em-up games). Donkey Kong had four screens with completely different ladder-and-platform layouts, variations in the graphics for most of the objects, different obstacles and hazards, and slightly different strategies needed on each screen. There was also a basic cut-scene interlude introducing each screen, another new feature we hadn't seen before.

As with all those early video games, squeezing more than sixty seconds of entertainment out of each 10p game involved getting better at the game. The difference with Donkey Kong, compared to Asteroids, for example, was that there were generic tactics for mastering the basic controls and timing, and tactics specific to individual elements of each of the four separate screens.

For example, on screen one it was the ladder-climbing and barrel-jumping, but on screen two there were horizontal conveyor-belt platforms that needed a totally different set of tactics. Jump timing had to be revised considerably depending on the direction the conveyor belt was moving. Level three was my favourite DK screen. It had a meandering route upwards on treacherous platforms, vertically travelling elevators, and deadly bouncing springs that introduced the concept of reaching a perilously narrow safe spot and patiently waiting to make your urgent, stressed-out sprint to the next safe spot.

Grabbing hard-to-reach objects to optionally boost your score was a risky proposition but the mark of a true Donkey Kong master. Providing you didn't mess it up and get whacked by a bouncing spring.

It was possible to make significant improvements in your Donkey Kong progress and high-scores by watching other people playing the game. Better players would know optimal routes and safe spots that you would otherwise have to figure out by pumping loads of 10p coins into the machine, and even by watching worse players you could study enemy paths and timings more effectively than when actually playing the game. This meant that a seemingly impossible hazard, for example the spring bouncing across the high platform on screen three, could be rendered almost a triviality after seeing a good player casually slip into the safe spot before making a perfectly timed run to the end of the level.

Duplicating what you had seen someone else do in Donkey Kong, with its fixed timings and mostly predictable enemies, was much easier than becoming a skilled spaceship pilot in Asteroids. That's not to say Donkey Kong was an easy game, but there were various elements of the gameplay that could be learned quickly and easily from other people. These days, we do the same things with far more complex games than Donkey Kong by watching YouTube gameplay videos and reading walkthroughs.

There were books full of arcade game tips 'n' tricks published in the early eighties but we didn't have time to go to WHSmiths or John Menzies to buy books, let alone read any of those books, because we were too busy playing arcade games in pubs, cafés and smoke-filled arcades.

On the last day of my second year in the sixth form, in the summer of 1981, I jumped out of the first-floor common room window. Nobody else had done this before, presumably because nobody else was quite that stupid. Before the official jump from the common room window, I had a practice go out of the window of an empty classroom on the opposite side of the sixth-form building. The area outside that classroom was mostly hidden from general view by adjacent walls, so the practice jump was as discreet as possible.

Sadboy stood outside to capture the attempt on his camera while a couple of other sixth-form kids watched from the room where I was making my exit. It wasn't my first jump from height but the landing surface was hard asphalt, not too different from a road, or any other playground in the early eighties.

The large windows were the type where the whole bottom half of the pane could be slid up and locked in place behind the top half, giving a gap about a yard wide and two feet high, so they were ideal for jumping access.

I climbed out and sat on the ledge with my feet hanging down on the outside. I called down to Sadboy to check he was ready. I could see him grinning up at me from behind his camera. I said "Okay," and pushed off, turning side-on to the building as I dropped from the first floor to the ground, landing on my feet and rolling forward into a clumsy somersault in an attempt to reduce the force of the impact on my ankles.

Sadboy was laughing and asking me if I was okay as I stood up. All I wanted to know was that he'd got the photo. He had, but I didn't see it for a couple of weeks because Sadboy used Truprint, which involved sending the film to them and getting your photos back in the post at a later date. Given the ancient camera technology involved, and only one chance to get the shot, Sadboy's photo of my practice jump was exceptionally good, freezing the moment when I was in mid fall, halfway between the first-floor window and the ground.

With the practice attempt an injury-free success, I was ready for the real jump. I remember the common room being really busy that day, lots of kids hanging around because they weren't in lessons and not many of the ones from my year doing much studying on the last day before the A-level exam period started.

There were two windows in the wall behind the pool table. I leaned against the radiator under the left window and casually slid the lower pane all the way up. Some of the girls scowled at me because they didn't want the window open. A few kids started to take an interest because Sadboy and I had been talking about the window jump for a couple of weeks, and the witnesses to the practice attempt had already been telling their friends about it.

I sat on the radiator and looked out at the playground, quiet during lessons with only a couple of late kids hurrying across it to a class. I didn't want to shuffle out onto the ledge this time because I wanted the jump to be more dramatic than the practice drop. Sadboy was getting a crowd together, telling them I was going to jump. I nodded at the dubious kids. "Yeah, I'm doing it. I'm going right now."

I looked out, down at the weathered grey tarmac. Chalk squares for hopscotch off to the left, beneath rows of windows on the side of the older redbrick classrooms of the original school building.

The common-room crowd had grown, and it looked as big as it was going to get. Another fifteen seconds and they'd start to lose interest and drift away, because some muppet sitting on a radiator saying he's going to jump out of a window isn't going to hold a crowd for more than a couple of minutes.

I said, "See ya," and I vaulted straight out, no cautious

preamble, no legs dangling tentatively over the edge. I'd done the drop once and I knew what it was going to feel like when I hit the ground.

I don't remember the fall but I remember hearing girls screaming above and behind me, and I was already laughing and cheering myself on as I rolled on the ground, got to my feet and legged it away around the corner towards the door at the back of the sixth-form block.

A year later, some kids came up to me in a pub in Ross, budding local hardmen, and they told me one of their tough-guy pals had jumped out of the window of the sixth-form block because he'd heard I'd done it the year before. I said it was a shame he hadn't been the first to do it, because that might have been pretty cool.

Chapter 3
Musical Interlude One
'What's another word for concern?'

Motorheads's Ace of Spades album was released on the eighth of November, 1980. I bought it a couple of weeks later, not from Round Ear Records but from the record department in John Menzies in Hereford. Some of the older shops in Hereford had basement levels, and the record department of John Menzies was in what they called the lower ground floor. I bought the Ace of Spades album on gold vinyl, despite being warned that the sound quality was worse than on the regular black vinyl version. It wasn't as if subtle fluctuations in the mid-range were going to be noticeable on my cheap late-seventies stereo system, particularly with an album like that being played as loud as I could possibly play it.

Some of my friends didn't understand why I'd bought the album, because I was into punk rock, and Motorhead was a heavy metal band. Many years later, we all know Motorhead inadvertently bridged the gap between heavy metal and punk but, back when it was actually happening, I didn't know anything more than it was a completely brilliant album, a relentless onslaught of full-speed clamour and in-your-face attitude, totally ballad-free and demanding repeat plays. Some tracks are overlooked now, forgotten not because they were weak filler, which they definitely were not, but because so many of the other tracks were stand-out masterpieces from a genre that was defining itself while we sat and listened, shell-shocked by the barrage of perfect noise. It was a great album to blast on a car's cassette player, outstanding motivational accompaniment to an Asteroids session in the record shop mini-arcade.

My friend Rob wasn't into Motorhead as much as me, but he always knew about the second-wave UK punk groups and the hardcore American bands before I did, and he got me into a lot of bands I might otherwise never have heard about, like Black Flag and Bad Brains.

We formed Unknown Soldier because we wanted to start a punk band. Listening to records by bands like Discharge and Black Flag it was clear to us that all we needed to do was get some cheap instruments and start making a godawful din. Neither of us could play an instrument, so Rob decided he was going to be the singer and I told my parents I wanted a bass guitar for my birthday. Bass was the obvious choice for me because I was infatuated with the Stranglers' bass sound and a bass looked a lot easier to play than a normal guitar. I ended up with a very cheap copy of a Rickenbacker and a crappy combo amplifier, and I learned to play classic punky basslines such as 'Warhead' by the UK Subs and 'Peaches' by The Stranglers.

At first, we couldn't find anyone else to join Unknown Soldier. Sadboy didn't want to be in the band so Rob told him he was our manager and had to get us gigs, despite the fact we couldn't play and didn't have a drummer or a guitarist. Those were trivialities we were certain we could overcome.

One evening I was at Smiley's house with Rob and Sadboy, and we were attempting to do band stuff which mostly involved leeching Smiley's coffee and calling him a 'turkey wanker'. Smiley lived near a turkey farm so he was called Turkey some of the time, and it was widely rumoured that he did part-time work artificially inseminating the turkeys.

Smiley quickly got fed up with me and Rob and he exiled us to a tiny room that was barely more than a storage cupboard. This resulted in a cassette recording featuring an angry, raging tirade of a song, the lyrics permanently burned into my long-term memory:

Locked in a room with lots of dog food,
Cans of Wesson oil,
I'm going to kill your fucking dog,
I'm going to shag your fucking Gran.

The next significant attempt at breaking into the big-time of anarcho-punk was a recording session in my parents' kitchen while they were on holiday. Rob, Sadboy and Smiley were there, and Smiley had brought a cousin who he assured us was a good guitar player. Of course, there was no guitar available so we never found out if this was true. Instead, Rob decided we should record a bass-and-vocals cover version of Discharge's 'Decontrol'. He hit an insurmountable obstacle almost immediately when he found he couldn't sing the line about only showing concern when war is declared. After a few failed attempts, he asked the question which became our standard retort in any confusing or awkward situation: "What's another word for concern?".

Sadboy attempted to help out by offering "anguish" as an alternative, but Rob decided it would be more fun to start an abusive singalong targeting Smiley, and the recording session faded out in a dismal anti-climax.

Chapter 4

Adventures in the real world
'What's that man doing, Daddy?'

I had all my driving lessons in Monmouth, in a cherry coloured Nissan Cherry with an independent driving instructor called Ken. He figured something out that my A-level teachers never managed to, or didn't bother to because I was such a lazy sod, and that was the fact that I responded far better to sarcasm and ridicule than I did to any form of positive encouragement to improve. These days, there's probably a law preventing reverse-psychology driving tuition, most likely there's a whole stack of laws to protect fragile learner-driver egos from the justifiably abusive retorts of frustrated, intolerant driving instructors.

In addition to taking the piss out of my driving ability, Ken would tell me to pull over to the side of the road, and I'd sit there for a few minutes waiting for the next instruction to do a three-point turn or reverse around a corner, while he watched a group of sixth-formers from Monmouth girls' school walking past on the pavement.

My driving test was booked for the first of April 1981.

One of the local mutants at The Moon, a sullen, acne-ravaged zombie farmhand called Igor Watkins, also had his test booked on that day. "April fool's day, so one of us is bound to fail," he told me, with the charisma-free self-confidence of the truly clueless.

Ken wasn't sure I was going to be ready, so we postponed my test for a month. I didn't tell anyone until after the first of April had been and gone, but plenty of people took great pleasure in telling me about Igor and his totally unexpected failure. Next time I saw him, I innocently asked him how he had done on his test, and then told him I'd postponed mine because I knew I wasn't ready for it. "You were absolutely right about April Fool's Day, weren't you?" I said to him, enjoying it a lot more than I should have.

My rescheduled test ended up taking place at the tail-end of a week of extremely heavy rain. The test centre in Monmouth was on the flood-plain close to the river and it already had an ankle-deep moat forming around it when Ken dropped me off after a final pre-test driving lesson. I don't remember much about the test itself, but I do clearly remember arriving back outside the test centre where the tester and I sat in the car watching local Sea Scouts paddling around in canoes outside the building, which was by then a yard deep in muddy flood water, while hapless driving-instructor types leaned out of first-floor windows asking if they might possibly be rescued sometime soon.

"I'm pleased to tell you, you've passed, Mr Tapper," the tester said. He wouldn't give me a lift anywhere and Ken was busy with his next driving lesson, probably a sixth-former from the girls' school, so I walked seven miles home with a big smile on my face the whole way because I'd passed my driving test the first time, and you only get one chance to do that. It felt like the most impressive video game high score ever. I didn't have a car, but that wasn't the point. Passing first time was the point.

I didn't get a car until late in 1982 when I started a foundation year at the art college in Hereford. I hadn't done art since the third year at grammar school, mostly because I had no artistic skills at all. I couldn't paint, couldn't draw, and I had no idea how sculpture worked.

I'd made a half-decent wooden salad bowl and a couple of skateboard decks in woodwork at school but that wasn't art, at least not according to the pretentious hippies who had to approve my application to join their college. I told them I wanted to do photography, although at the time I didn't have a proper camera. They wanted to know why I hadn't done O-level or A-level art. I said I'd done a bit of technical drawing as part of Design and Technology in school but that just made them scowl and go quiet. In a flash of inspired initiative, I fabricated a sorry tale of how I'd wanted to do Art at O-level but my parents had told me to concentrate on academic topics and I didn't have enough time to fit anything arty into my school timetable. Somehow, this flimsy, transparent bullshit nonsense not only worked but set a standard for the whole year I spent at art college.

The foundation course was supposed to be two years, but

I joined the start of the second year. I have no idea how that happened, I really don't. I think it might have been possible for someone with an A-level portfolio comparable to the next Picasso, but I had nothing. No portfolio, no art qualifications, no camera, not even an A4 pad full of scribbled pictures of exploding tanks and helicopters that looked like they'd been drawn by a disturbed child. Well, yes, I did have an A4 pad just like that, but I didn't tell them about it.

To get from Garway to art college in Hereford I needed a car, but my father bought me an orange four-door Lada instead. The Lada was a Fiat built in Russia, presumably by terminally unhappy peasants with no previous experience of manufacturing cars. I asked the salesman why it came with a starting handle and he assured me it was 'just part of the package'. He should have applied to go to art college because he had the bullshit nonsense completely down.

Turning the key to start the engine would randomly not work, for no apparent reason other than to justify the existence of the starting handle. One time, while I was hand-cranking the engine in a car park in Monmouth, a family with a young son walked past.

"What's that man doing, daddy?" asked the toddler.

"It's Russian," I told them. "They all have to be started like this."

The cable between the accelerator pedal and the carburettor snapped while I was overtaking a lorry on the quiet B-road out near the Duke of Wellington pub. One advantage of having a car only marginally beyond Flintstones technology was the ease of DIY corrective maintenance. The light in the boot had never worked, so I ripped the wiring out and used an eighteen-inch length of it to replace the snapped throttle cable. After I'd fixed the cable, the engine idled faster but the car's top speed also increased by twenty miles per hour.

I had my earliest encounters with home video games while I was at art college. The first one was Pong on an Atari console at the house of one of the other students, a rich kid with a sports car and whose father was a surgeon. They lived in a massive house with a tennis court in the garden, but I was more impressed by the gadget that let him play video games without leaving his own home. He was one of the more down-to-earth kids at art college, apart from the Atari console and the sports car and the tennis court, and he was there because he had artistic talent. I still didn't have any, and I never would.

I borrowed a 35mm SLR from Rob and I took photographs of rusty garden tools and road-kill. The lecturers were more interested in the trippy bullshit students could dream up to describe their work, rather than the work itself, and I quickly figured this out and exploited it as much as possible.

One of my friends there was Chris Morgan, who I'd met when we were both in the first year of the sixth form in Ross. He left the sixth form to go to art college, the same year I'd had to stay in school to re-sit my failed A-levels. He didn't understand how I'd managed to join the second year of the foundation course but he was happy to see me there. He was an amazing artist but the lecturers didn't like his work because the pictures he painted were almost photorealistic. I heard one of them telling him, "That's not art, it's illustration," and they meant it as a negative criticism, as if outstanding talent alone was meaningless without a pile of pretentious twaddle around it.

For some reason, the college attendance hours included staying until eight o'clock in the evening every Wednesday. There was a signing-out book that wasn't available until about five to eight, so we couldn't just go home early or that's what most of us would have done. The lecturers usually all left between five and six so most of the time we'd wait until the coast was clear, walk to the nearest pub and go back to college at eight to sign out and go home.

If something prevented us walking to the pub, for example heavy rain or a lurking lecturer, we'd play a game of increasingly ridiculous dares and forfeits instead. Particularly memorable incidents include Chris eating a page out of a glossy magazine as a forfeit, and a dare which involved me going outside and knocking on the unlocked glass doors of the college until a cleaner opened the unlocked glass door and asked what the hell was wrong with me.

The other early encounter with home video games came via a student called Raggety and his ZX Spectrum. Raggety was a heavy smoker, as were many of the art school students. He kept his habit going at minimal cost by collecting stubbed-out dog-ends from ashtrays and anywhere outdoors where someone had dropped the last half-inch of a cigarette on the ground. He'd extract the remaining tobacco from a dozen or so scavenged dog-ends and make a roll-up from them.

Raggety lived not far off my route home from college so it was convenient to give him a lift, even more convenient when it meant I could spend time with his ZX Spectrum. Seeing a computer in someone's house was a total revelation, an apex event in my life. It was at once exhilarating and overwhelming. The possibilities were infinite. It was a glimpse of the gleaming chrome-and-jetpacks future we'd been promised in cartoons and B-movies since the fifties, a mind-blowing concept, and it was right there on top of a dusty desk in Raggety's folks' front room. I asked the only question I was ever going to ask in a situation like that. "Have you got any games for it?"

We played Arcadia first, a mashup plagiarism of various arcade game shooters and my introduction to the retina-melting colour-clash flicker of Spectrum games. Being able to play it over and over without spending any money or being jostled by ruddy-cheeked, dead-eyed, pint-wielding farm labourers was a threshold moment.

Most of the time we played The Hobbit, a text adventure with static graphic representations of significant locations. Nothing to shoot, but plenty to think about. Puzzles and choices, where the slightest wrong decision or poorly constructed sentence could kill you all the way back to the last time you saved the game.

A door was opening right there in front of me, a round

green door in a comfortable tunnel, while Thorin sat down and started singing about gold and Raggety rolled another dog-end cigarette. The worlds on either side of the screen were overlaying each other in a way the Spectrum's colour palette never could.

I spent countless hours in the land of Middle Earth in Raggety's house. We got stuck in the goblin dungeon for days, concocting outlandish methods of stringing various words together in an attempt to resolve the problem during lunch breaks at art college. Nobody else knew what we were talking about. Our adventures within the game were an alien concept because nobody else had a computer at home; none of our fellow students were spending hours in a text-based virtual Middle Earth trying to figure out how to progress beyond a single-screen image of a dungeon.

Raggety would take a long, thoughtful draw on a stinking, recycled tar stick before asking me what I thought Thorin might be doing when he wasn't singing about gold. We knew he was in there, existing virtually while we stared at the same picture of a dungeon for hours, and we knew he must be doing something because he had become more real to us than anyone who had given up trying to talk to us in college. Thorin repeatedly sang about gold as we repeatedly failed to type the correct sequence of words that would allow us to move to the next location in the game. There was no internet to trawl for a solution, no online walkthrough available, only our relentless quest to succeed.

I had no comparable quest for success in the real world,

although various disconnected aspects of my life were levelling up independently since the introduction of a car. Rob and I convinced a guitarist and drummer to join Unknown Soldier and we were regularly rehearsing in the village hall a few hundred yards away from Rob's house. Towards the end of 1982 I spent most Sunday evenings watching Hart to Hart with a friendly weed-smoking bleached-blonde in the lounge of her parents' house. To her credit, she never once laughed at my Lada.

The art college sent the second-year foundation-course students on a trip to the Tate gallery in London in early 1983, where the pretentious bullshit reached its peak. The accompanying lecturers dismissed our enthusiasm for massive, genuinely impressive oil paintings of horses-versus-artillery warfare, and attempted to convince us that 'real art' involved single-colour canvasses with random, nonsensical titles - "Just think for a moment what the artist is telling you" - and paintings that looked like someone had tipped ketchup on a cat and thrown it at the canvas - "Those unique aesthetic qualities can never be reproduced exactly". Art, bullshit and gullibility, forever intertwined.

I was rapidly losing interest in art, even though I was also rapidly realising I could easily bullshit my way through a potentially lucrative artistic career. In the end I played them at their own game, walked away with my integrity intact, and final proof they were a bunch of soulless hypocrites.

Hereford art college used a promotional message that everyone who passed their foundation course got offered a place on a university or polytechnic degree course. The truth, which I suspected from about halfway through the year, was the facts were reversed. The college didn't divulge the details of foundation course passes or failures until all the responses were received from the universities and polytechnics. They only passed the foundation course students who were offered places on degree courses. Chances were, if you were good enough to be offered a place on a degree course, you'd have passed the foundation course anyway. What they didn't want were students who weren't offered degree courses being on the list of passes at Hereford art college, because that would mean they couldn't use the hundred-percent record in their marketing material.

I half-heartedly applied for a few photography degree courses and I was asked to attend an interview at Stoke-on-Trent Poly. I went up on a train with my portfolio of unimaginative, technically mediocre, self-developed black-and-white photos of trees and garden tools, gave them a straight-up admission that I absolutely wasn't interested in arty bullshit, and a few weeks later they sent me a formal offer of a place on a photography degree course. All I can think is the degree course must have been massively undersubscribed that year. Maybe they were eligible for a special grant by offering a place to someone with no discernible artistic ability. Maybe they were simply bowled over by my honesty. Whatever the reason, I was offered a place there and it came as a total shock. I'd gone through the motions of applying and attending the interview but I fully expected to be turned down.

I didn't want to spend three years in Stoke taking photos of dead cats and giving the pictures pretentious titles. I didn't want to move away from Unknown Soldier and all my friends. I panicked, I suppose, because I was immature and scared. I hid the offer letter, told the art college in Hereford I hadn't been offered a place on a degree course anywhere, and they failed me for the foundation course, as I knew they would. Based on what I'd achieved while I was there, the failure was justified. I wasn't an artist and I never would be. Knowing the college would have passed me if I'd shown them the offer from Stoke just made me glad I was done with them and free of their pompous bullshit. Now all I had to do was figure out what I was going to try next.

After leaving art college in the summer of 1983, the first thing I absolutely had to do was get my own ZX Spectrum. It took a considerable amount of effort to convince my parents I needed a computer; they were not at all pleased that I'd wasted a year in art college and was now back in the same unemployed, oxygen-thieving situation I'd been in twelve months earlier, with nothing to show for my time in college except a wad of crappy photographs. There were a few moments when I wanted to show them the letter offering me a place at Stoke Poly, but I knew it would have just made the whole sorry mess a lot worse. Many years later I did tell them all about it, but they acted as if they couldn't even remember me going to art college. I suppose people have different priorities and perspectives, different ways of remembering the past and partitioning those memories into good, bad, and not worth the effort.

The Spectrum had been out for a year by the time I got mine, so there were already a hell of a lot of games available for it. I got The Hobbit as soon as I could, got stuck in the goblin dungeon equally quickly, and revived my virtual relationship with Thorin, who was nowhere near as much fun as he'd been when I was playing the game with Raggety. There were other games, lots and lots of other games, but there was one specific Spectrum game released in 1983 that grabbed me by the neck and hauled me up the next few rungs of the video-game-addiction ladder. Two words: Manic Miner.

I can see so many similarities now between that game and Motorhead's track 'Ace of Spades'. Initially jaw-dropping, phenomenally inspirational, subsequently played over and over until it became a parody of itself, listed in the top ten of everyone's favourite everything ever, fondly remembered by people who weren't even born when it was released, cited as a major event in the evolution of its respective field of entertainment, and still just as relevant today as it ever was. I'm eternally grateful to the combination of fate, chance and the space-time continuum for putting me on this planet during the period when both of those glorious life-changers were created.

Manic Miner wasn't a game for the toe-dippers, the Two-Go Charlies, the lightweights who'd give up in frustration after dying on a simple jump over one of the hazardous plants on the first screen.

In common with the vast majority of early home

computer games, Manic Miner was unapologetically hardcore, with a small quota of lives, no option to save progress or continue from anywhere other than the start of the game when all your lives were gone, and a relentlessly high level of difficulty. Even games that looked soft, like Horace goes Skiing, were brutal sledgehammers waiting to pummel the faces of the unwary.

Manic Miner was twenty screens of fail-fail-try-again, willpower-challenging platform-gaming awesomeness. Of course, you get people today posting single-life emulator speedrun completions of Manic Miner on YouTube, but none of that takes anything away from those of us who were the first to face the challenge alone on black-and-white portable television sets with no previous experience of pixel-perfect, microsecond-timed leaps over animated toilets and mutant clockwork-duck monsters.

Honestly, there were only two types of platform game on the Spectrum; there was Manic Miner and there was everything that came after it. Wanted: Monty Mole was arguably more polished and varied, but it will never be anything more than another mine-themed platform game that trailed in the wake of the mighty Manic Miner. Even the true sequel, Jet Set Willy, which was a Metroidvania game before there were any Metroid or Castlevania games, couldn't topple its predecessor from the throne.

JSW set a few precedents for much-hyped blockbuster gaming releases: copy protection that was annoying but fairly easy to bypass, game-breaking bugs, cover-up bullshit from the publishers, in this case "Those aren't bugs, they're deliberate features", and the subsequent hiring by the publishers of a player who fixed the bugs in order to complete the otherwise broken game. And we were still just under thirty years away from Skyrim's release date.

Manic Miner will always be in my top ten favourite Spectrum games, not occupying a specific spot because I change my mind about the order of my top tens on a daily basis. Other games that are definitely in my top ten (at the time I'm writing this sentence) are: The Lords of Midnight, the Spectrum conversion of arcade game Commando, Chuckie Egg, Jetpac, Knight Lore, The Way of The Exploding Fist, Uridium, and Barbarian. If one of your favourites isn't in that list, it's possibly because I never played it. I didn't play every Spectrum game ever released, and I doubt any one person ever has.

A lesser-known Spectrum game called Cauldron had platform game elements plus horizontally scrolling shooter sequences where you rode a broomstick and dodged various cartoon horror enemies. I flooded my parents' kitchen while I was playing Cauldron and, for once, the real-world memories of taking up the soaking carpet tiles and putting them outside on the patio to dry are more vivid than my memories of the game. Learn from my mistake: don't leave a kitchen sink filling up with water while you grab thirty seconds on a video game. Those seconds will turn into minutes and your kitchen floor will turn into the obligatory swamp level from every CRPG since the dawn of time.

Cauldron didn't introduce any ground-breaking gameplay concepts but it was a decent attempt at mixing up a couple of established genres.

Quite a few other Spectrum games definitely introduced ground-breaking concepts, contributing significantly to video game evolution. Knight Lore by Ultimate (who went on to become Rare) is probably the one that went further, at the time, than any other game, when it came to defying the limitations of the Spectrum hardware while simultaneously defining a genre. The three-dimensional isometric perspective, with objects moving seamlessly in front of other objects, was not natively supported and had to be handled by a custom image-masking technique devised by the developers. Of course, I didn't know anything about that at the time, I just played the game.

The Ultimate games came in glossy cardboard cases about the same size as a DVD movie case, although DVD movie cases were still more than ten years in the future when Knight Lore was released in 1984. The Ultimate games also cost more than most games, retailing for £9.95 when the majority of decent Spectrum games were about a fiver.

Barbarian: The Ultimate Warrior was the first game I can remember that had controversially gory content overshadowed by protests about the scandalous image of a Page Three girl in a bikini on the packaging, and it ended up getting banned in Germany, which was no surprise to anyone. The bloke dressed as the Barbarian on the game box was the same guy who eventually became Wolf on the UK Gladiators TV show.

The Lords of Midnight didn't get banned anywhere, despite being heavily 'inspired by' The Lord of The Rings. It was another Spectrum game that defied all expectations, creating a believable pseudo-three-dimensional world, blending a solo quest with a turn-based military strategy game, and it came in a large-format cardboard box with a £9.95 price tag and a scene-setting novella. It was an amazing game, a totally absorbing experience. I first beat it with Morkin on his Frodo-esque quest to destroy the Ice Crown, and I finally achieved a crushing, steamroller military victory after countless botched attempts. Twenty years later, I wrote a retrospective review of The Lords of Midnight for Edge magazine.

Meanwhile, still in 1983, back in the real world, I realised I could get a job messing about with computers. Two years earlier, playing pool while I waited to screw up my A-levels, I hadn't even seen a computer. I knew they existed, in the same way I knew multi-millionaire supermodels existed, but I had never considered the possibility of interacting with one.

Before I could spend the rest of my life messing about with computers, I knew I needed some kind of qualification related to computing. Hereford was unable to provide the type of computer course I was looking for, so I went over the border into Wales to take a two-year BTEC course in Computer Studies at Allt-yr-yn college in Newport. The course was quite new, and they were still struggling to define the curriculum for computer studies, which meant there was a maths class with a tutor who was constantly frustrated by a room full of maths dunces, an accounting class with a tutor who clearly didn't want to be there, and a communication class with a right-on hippy called Mary.

I was older than most of the other students on the Computer Studies course because they had come straight onto it after leaving the fifth form at secondary school. I don't remember them all, but a few will always stick in my mind. Craig could walk on his hands, the Fricker twins were called Richard and Peter (I bet they really thanked their parents for that), Steven underlined everything twice in red, Russell had a ZX81 and an American accent, and Dean was the inspirational revelation who introduced me to 'Brainbomb' by Punishment of Luxury, got me into weight training and taught me how to juggle.

Dean lived in High Cross, only a minute or two off my daily hour-long route to college, and after a few weeks we fell into an informal arrangement where I picked him up in the morning and dropped him off on my way home. I was fairly compensated with coffee, biscuits, music by bands I'd never heard of, and a fresh take on everything from throwing knives to getting a business start-up grant to build a recording studio in his father's garage.

In the second year of college we all had Wednesday afternoons off, ostensibly to study, and most Wednesday afternoons I'd go into town with Dean to buy records or go to the cinema. We watched a double-bill of Mad Max and Mad Max 2 but they showed the second film first, which has always stuck in my mind as being a bit daft, and we saw The

Terminator, which was astoundingly brilliant at the time, and will always be one of my favourite films.

There was far less actual computer work than I expected from a course called Computer Studies. We wrote a few rudimentary COBOL programs, but most of the time we were in non-computing lectures being bad at maths or laughing at incomprehensible accounting methods.

The college common room had a Zaxxon machine near the pool table. Zaxxon was another game, like Defender, that looked like the sort of game I wanted to be good at, but wasn't.

Steven, in addition to underlining everything twice in red, was the first person I ever met who had a home-computing superiority complex. He found my ownership of a ZX Spectrum to be truly hilarious, as it was clearly vastly inferior to his Atari 800. After a few months of being told on a daily basis that the Spectrum was bad, that all Spectrum games were rubbish, that I'd made a colossal mistake buying a Spectrum, and that the Atari 800 was so much better than a Spectrum that I wouldn't be able to cope with the experience, I asked Steven if I could have a look at it. I had to trade him a lift home from college as part of the bargain but it seemed like a fair deal to me. At the time.

However, the chance to 'have a look at' his godlike games machine and its extensive library of incomparably perfect games turned out to be just that. I had to sit and watch him play game after game, with no offer of actually having a go on any of them, and no offer of a coffee or even a glass of squash.

First up, BC's Quest for Tires, complete with the American spelling of tyres. I can only judge what I saw, of course, because I wasn't given the opportunity to play it, but it looked like a straightforward scrolling game of jump-timing and hazard-dodging. The graphics were different from Spectrum graphics, no argument there, but this wasn't the brain-melting experience I'd been promised. I watched Steven trundling the caveman across the screen a few times, bouncing over dents in the ground and ducking under trees, and I thought it looked like Moon Patrol because the gameplay was virtually identical. As an opening act to astound a Spectrum owner, it wasn't the game I would have chosen.

In fact, out of all the games I had to sit and watch, the only other one I can even remember, let alone feel like I was missing out on by not being able to play it, was Spelunker. It looked great, a mine-themed platform game with all sorts of dangers lurking in the cramped corridors, exactly the kind of game I would have enjoyed playing.

The Atari 800 had better graphics technology than the Spectrum, but seeing Steven's Atari didn't make me want to own one. Spectrum coders were constantly producing games that exceeded the hardware's limitations, creating classics of imaginative gameplay that would define genres and keep me playing games on that flickering, squeaking, rubber-keyed toy computer for the next few years.

Chapter 5

Normal service will never be resumed
'Prepare to joust, buzzard bait!'

The Ross Spur service stations either side of the A449 dual carriageway at Ross-On-Wye were our Sunday afternoon destination of choice for most of the eighties. Don't bother going there to take a nostalgic look because the original service stations were demolished in 2001, with nowadays only a motorway-prices Starbucks on the southbound side, and a KFC opposite.

The original Ross Spur service stations, much like most of the pubs in the eighties, had their own character. I'd even go as far as to say they had their own unique charm, and most importantly they had video games.

The southbound service station only ever had room for one game cabinet in the small front foyer, but they had a run of consistently decent games. Memorable upright cabinets we played there include Tron, Black Tiger, Mr Do!, Mr Do's Castle, and Crush Roller, which I never saw anywhere else.

Tron was a decent mix of several different games. There was the obligatory light-cycle death race, a maze game with tanks, a sequence where you had to destroy the enemy CPU by aiming your flailing arm with the weird rotary control knob, and a fourth game mode I can't remember. I wasn't very good at Tron and I'd like to blame the unique experience of the annoying rotary control knob for that.

Black Tiger was a hard game. I can only imagine it was devised by someone for whom Ghosts 'n Goblins felt far too easy. "I know," they said, "let's make everything lethal, even the ground. You want treasure chests that burst into deadly flames when you open them? You've got it. Tricky jumps between narrow columns over pits of certain death, with snakes wrapped around the columns and unreachable enemies throwing crap at you at the same time? Here you go." We kept playing it despite the crazy frustration level, and we started calling one-pound coins 'zenny coins' after the in-game currency. Black Tiger let you play as a character who looked like Conan the Barbarian but behaved like an acrophobic masochist having a stroke, and it wasn't the last game to do this. I sometimes load it up on MAME, just to remind myself how tough it was, and I'm still not very good at it.

Mr Do! was pure genius, and will always be one of my favourite arcade games, forever in my top ten of all time. Everything about it suggested the designers were seriously abusing mind-expanding pharmaceuticals. The protagonist was a clown, or at least he was wearing something that looked like a red-and-white clown suit, armed with a bouncing ball that was supposed to return after he threw it but, more often than not, it got stuck around a corner or behind a giant apple. Those giant apples could be pushed into vertical shafts to fall on an unwary monster, unless the monster ate the apple. At intervals that weren't as random as we first thought, a monster that was a big capital letter E, or X, or T, or R, or A, would emerge at the top of the screen and start marching around the maze. Cherries, in mathematically perfect groups of eight, could be collected by the clown for more points, unless a monster ate them first. Slices of cake and other items that looked edible appeared in the middle of the maze, luring the greedy player with the promise of some more points. Sometimes, but infrequently enough to remain an almost mythical occurrence, a diamond would materialise somewhere in the maze. We were so shocked to see this when it actually happened that we would yell and point, promising unyielding devotion to the game, and then die due to being hopelessly distracted by the diamond before ever managing to collect it.

Mr Do's Castle was a different genre of game, hardly anything in common with Mr Do! apart from the clown-suited protagonist being chased by monsters. If Mr Do! was the maze-game collect-em-up mutant son of Pac-Man and Dig Dug, then Mr Do's Castle was the bastard offspring of Space Panic, Donkey Kong and yet another bucketload of military-grade hallucinogenics. The pursuing monsters were more relentless than ever, hurtling around the claustrophobic platforms-and-ladders levels and morphing into faster, more aggressive versions accompanied by a suitably ominous sound effect. Ladders could be pushed to delay the monsters or influence their routes around the screen, and traps could be dug to eliminate them, but every action needed a degree of forward planning, or disaster was inevitable. Sadboy was good at Mr Do's Castle, probably his favourite arcade game of all time.

Crush Roller didn't have a protagonist clown or a giant letter E chasing you up and down ladders, but it was definitely another game developed by crazy people on drugs. The basic concept of changing the colour of the traversable areas of the screen was popularised in the far more well-known Q*bert a year later, but Crush Roller did it first and did it with gleefully deranged enthusiasm. According to online information, Crush Roller was only called Crush Roller in Japan, but it was definitely called Crush Roller in the southbound Ross Spur service station. The player controlled a paintbrush, navigating a post-Pac-Man style maze in an attempt to change the colour of the paths throughout the maze. Thwarting your decorating progress were enemies that looked a bit like fish, capable of killing the paintbrush by touching it, and non-lethal animals that tracked paw prints through painted areas, which meant you had to go back and paint over those parts of the path, optionally running over the animal for some bonus points. The titular crush rollers were a couple of power-up paint rollers that you could propel along a predefined length of path to run over and temporarily remove one or both of the enemy fish. I never saw a Crush Roller cabinet anywhere else, which was a bit of a shame because it was a fun game.

The only video game I remember playing in the service station on the northbound side of Ross Spur was Joust. Put simply, Joust was an unbelievably brilliant game. The premise sounds just as bonkers as many of the other games of that era - heroic knights on flying ostriches fighting bad guys on buzzards over a lake of lava, with occasional visits by a supposedly unkillable pterodactyl - but there was a sense of legendary sobriety about the whole thing, from the challenging words displayed at the start of a game - Prepare to joust, buzzard bait! - to the restrained presentation, and the bizarrely realistic movement of the minimally animated birds. The absolute clincher, the element that raised it above the majority of games we were playing, quite a few years before we saw Gauntlet or Smash TV, was the simultaneous two-player mode. As pioneers of this revolutionary gameplay, we knew we had a responsibility to future generations of gamers by our defining actions, so we did what we had to do to set a blueprint for player etiquette in all multiplayer games to come: we blamed the other player for every death we suffered, and we reneged without warning on our promise not to shove them off the edge of the platform into the fiery claws of the lurking lava troll when they only had one life left.

Café Ascari in Hereford, which almost everybody called Ascari's, and which Sadboy only ever referred to as Ask Gary's, had a tabletop Scramble followed by a tabletop Galaga. In my first crime novel, Cold Inside, I relocated Ascari's to Hull and renamed it Gaspari's but I kept the tabletop Galaga and the pressed-foil early-eighties ashtrays. I haven't been in Ascari's since the late eighties so my memories of the place are fixed in that era, like a set of fading photographs in a time capsule. I always seemed to end up in Ascari's, whether I was alone or wandering around town with my friends. There were other cafés in Hereford, but they were either full of old grannies or they didn't have any video games.

Scramble was the first horizontally scrolling shoot-em-up I ever played. It took place in a sequence of increasingly difficult zones, but there was no pause or transition between the distinctly different areas, you just kept on flying while the environmental graphics and hazards dynamically changed as you progressed through the game. There were two fire buttons, one for a forward-firing gun and the other for dropping bombs. The spaceship you were flying was constantly using up fuel; the method of refuelling was the first instance of this illogical but weirdly intuitive video game trope: destroy fuel depots to replenish your own fuel supply. I never got obsessively excited about Scramble, although it was a fun game and a considerable challenge, but I know I owe it eternal gratitude for leading the way for all the classic horizontally scrolling shooters that followed, from Gradius and R-Type to the Thunder Force series.

Compared to that lumbering, prehistoric ancestor of horizontally scrolling shooters, the next game in Ascari's was Galaga - released in 1981, the same year as Scramble - a slick, refined, evolutionary leap for vertical fixed shooters, light years beyond Space Invaders and its own direct ancestor from two years earlier, Galaxian. Colourful alien bugs flew onto the screen in choreographed formations, challenge levels offered the chance to dramatically boost your score, and there was the ultimate risk-versus-reward feature where you could allow one of the big aliens to abduct your ship with a tractor beam before attempting to retrieve the captured ship by shooting the alien next time it left the hovering ranks to spin and zig-zag its way down the screen. If you managed it, the retrieved ship would dock itself alongside your active ship, giving you double firepower until one or both ships were destroyed. The advantage of having two guns was offset by the distinct disadvantage of being twice as wide, and therefore twice as likely to be hit by alien fire or dive-bombing space bugs. Galaga had another new feature, a percentage rating of your shooting accuracy included with the score summary when your game ended. The percentage didn't add anything to the score but it was interesting to see, and it provided extra incentive to improve, particularly if it was low enough to earn a sarcastic slow handclap from your spectators.

Local cafés and service stations were perfect for an hour or two on a single game, but longer journeys to coastal towns meant not only a wider choice of video games but also the incomparable atmosphere of the beachfront arcades. From Herefordshire, the closest decent seaside arcades were at Weston-super-Mare, across the River Severn in Somerset, and The Mumbles on the Gower peninsula in Wales. Weston was marginally closer, but both were suitable for day-trips if we made an early start. Barry Island and Porthcawl were closer than The Mumbles but they were also a considerably grimmer prospect, although not entirely repellent enough to completely deter us from making an occasional trip.

There were a few big arcades at The Mumbles, one was near the pier and there were a couple in Oystermouth, a mile along the coastal road from the pier. I'd seen the arcades blossom from dingy slot-machine joints into vibrant, sensory-overload video game arcades during annual family summer holidays between 1977 and 1980. My parents would book a week in a holiday flat at Limeslade Bay, or a chalet at Caswell, in August, and we'd spend most of the days inside, looking out of the window at the rain. When they'd lost all patience with my griping about being bored, they'd let me walk to the pier arcade if we were in the flat at Limeslade, or they'd drive me there if we were in the Caswell chalet.

My parents called the arcade "The Pennies", as in "Do you want to go down The Pennies, John?" even when nothing in there cost less than 10p for a go, apart from the ancient games of chance, which were games of no-chance-at-all, but you didn't know this when you were only six years old, where pennies could be rolled down metal chutes towards sliding blocks where they would land on heaped piles of other pennies and lie there forever, and you ran out of pennies and started crying.

I saw a couple of the first video games in those arcades at Mumbles: Tail Gunner and Space Wars. I didn't play Space Wars because it was a two-player game with no option to play against a computer-controlled opponent, but I had a few goes on Tail Gunner, enough to decide that, at the time, slot machines and pinball were more fun than video games.

A typical day trip to Weston would start with a plan being made the previous weekend, or in the pub the night before the trip. This would usually be me and Sadboy deciding to get on the road before 7 a.m. so we could arrive at Weston early enough to nab a decent parking space close to the pier, and the rest of the potential Weston crew shaking their heads in appalled disbelief and telling us they'd meet us down there later.

Sometimes we'd manage to convince a couple of our friends that an early start was a really good idea and that they should come in the car with us, although it always seemed like the friends without their own cars were the easiest to convince.

We'd drive down to Monmouth, then through Chepstow, to get onto the M4 close to the Severn Bridge. We'd traditionally make a stop at Aust services on the far side of the bridge, supposedly for breakfast, but it always included a warm-up on whatever machines they had in the mini-arcade and a session of making loud noises in the traps of the public toilets. The more people involved in the trap-groaning, the better it sounded. Two people in a couple of separate cubicles could generate a mildly amusing back-and-forth commentary of grunts and cries for help, but additional participants turned it into a trap-opera of impressive stupidity. We peaked during a trip involving the Plunkett brothers, who hurled themselves into the fiasco with incredible enthusiasm and creativity, calling out radio chatter from a high-altitude bombing mission while others in attendance grunted, blew colossal raspberries, and ultimately collapsed in helpless laughing fits as the bombing run escalated in volume and profanity.

Classic shouts from the traps always included "Is that you, Gary?" in the style of a confused elder, and "Oh Christ, what's that smell?" in a strong Welsh-valleys accent. Walking out of the cubicle following a raucous bout of trap-groaning was always fun, acting like it was nothing to do with you while avoiding the reproving stares of sensible fathers accompanied by wide-eyed, traumatised toddlers.

Sadboy carried a black marker pen so he could reply to toilet-wall graffiti. He had two standard replies, one for invitations to meet up for romantic liaisons and extravagant claims of organ size: "Get a life grandad", and one for everything else: "God will make you pay for this".

After leaving Aust, more or less at 8 a.m. if we were sticking to the plan, we would take the scenic route on the A403 down to Avonmouth, get on the M5, and be parking up half an hour later on the mostly deserted seafront car park at Weston.

Tradition was a massive part of Sadboy's life, and he enforced it on everyone else with considerable zeal. First stop, always the pier. At the zenith of the Golden Age, there were open-fronted shacks full of video games along the sides of the pier, and a big arcade at the end of it. This was a long time before the pier was rebuilt in 2010 following the fire in 2008.

One of the problems with the crowded holiday resort arcades, apart from being crowded, was the high probability that the controls on the arcade game cabinets would be knackered due to the sheer volume of players and the generally disrespectful hammering they gave the machines. Another arcade gripe, and this was a particular annoyance for Sadboy, was you'd always get some gormless kid, with his face covered in chocolate or ketchup, trying to stick his head in front of you to look at the screen while you were playing a game. Sadboy would unsubtly elbow these kids in the side of the head while mimicking their constant chirping of "What you doing, mister?".

When we'd had a go on all the decent, least-knackered games on the pier, Sadboy would buy an ice cream cone from the stall at the front of it and ritually shove it into his own face, leaving the dripping splodge of ice cream there while we walked to the next arcade.

Despite us renaming it Weston-super-Nightmare, we had a lot of good times there and we played several games we never saw anywhere else. Two that instantly come to mind are Gauntlet and Smash TV, both rich sources of classic, multifunctional quotes. Gauntlet's "Someone shot the food" turned out to be appropriate in a variety of situations, from the blatantly obvious: a drunken friend knocking their pie and chips off a wall onto the pavement, to the remarkably surreal: a response given to an unsolicited phone call enquiring as to one's interest in taking out house insurance. "I've not seen such bravery" from the same game could be used almost anywhere, from witnessing a piss-head staggering out of the door of the takeaway to stubbing one's own toe and not screaming in agony.

Smash TV's most obvious quote was lifted word-for-word from Robocop, but it's easily the most versatile one I can think of: "I'd buy that for a dollar!". We also wore out "Big money, big prizes…I love it!" as both a genuine appreciation of a satisfying result, and as a sarcastic response to something monumentally disappointing.

As a day-trip coastal destination, Barry Island might seem like a likely candidate for monumental disappointment but it was deceptively entertaining back in the early eighties. The beach was a steeply sloping pile of pebbles, liberally daubed with pungent, rotting seaweed and aesthetically similar discarded prophylactics, and the car park looked like a good place to dump any old kitchen appliances you might have had hanging around on the pavement outside your 1920's terraced coal-miners' two-bedroom house with nicotine-yellowed lace curtains and a piece of cardboard covering one of the broken windows. I don't know anyone who went to Barry Island for their actual summer holidays but I'm guessing they were only marginally less miserable for the other fifty weeks of the year.

Our day-trips to Barry were the result of spontaneous coin-toss decisions, reckless dares, and doomed speculation: "Let's go to Barry and see if it's even more shit than last year", and it was close enough down the M4 to make the risk of monumental disappointment seem worthwhile, when there was always the chance of seeing someone get stranded on the big wheel.

The funfair at Barry Island was awful. I'm sure there was a sign there that said "Pleasure Beach" or something equally misleading. We'd pile into the ghost train on a couple of rattling, shaky death-trap carriages, armed with pockets full of pebbles from the rancid beach, and we'd pelt the shuddering, grime-encrusted ghosts and vampires while yelling an entire dictionary of swear words as loud as possible throughout the entire minute and a half of otherwise stagnant tedium. It was the logically natural evolution of the Aust services trap-operas, channelling our dismay at the lacklustre offerings of the funfair into a few short moments of violent, raging retribution directed at the most hopelessly unresponsive victims available. I felt a certain degree of remorse after, jumping out of the mine cart and asking the friends who had chosen to wait outside if they had heard any sounds of destruction and profanity while we were on the ride. "Yeah, it was really loud. Let's get out of here," was a typical response, accompanied by wary checks for approaching disgruntled fairground ride operators.

Abandoning the funfair, several small arcades could be found on the streets nearby, crammed in between chip shops and those open-fronted stalls full of crude cartoon postcards depicting drunken, sunburned perverts staring at unfeasibly curvy women in tiny bikinis while announcing painfully obvious double-entendres in speech bubbles that would have given Mary Whitehouse a triple coronary.

It was in one of those side-street arcades in Barry where I first played R-Type. The immediate thing you'll think of, if you ever played R-Type or watched someone else playing it, is the size of the end-of-level bosses. The first one is the most iconic: a gigantic, biomechanical monstrosity diligently paying homage to (and not blatantly stealing) HR Giger's classic alien design, complete with a chest-bursting alien popping out of the big one's guts. It's an easy fight, utterly trivial compared to almost anything that turned up in subsequent games, or even in subsequent levels of R-Type, but it's a genre-defining moment because that's exactly what it was. At the time, the level-one boss was inconceivably big, and terrifyingly difficult. It filled half the screen and it fired great big alien bullets all over the place, and it seemed mostly impervious to your attacks.

And, when you eventually managed to beat R-Type's level-one boss, level two was even harder, a claustrophobic organic corridor crammed with bursting spore pods, massive lobster-scorpion creatures, an unkillable metallic snake-thing and an end-of-level mutant anemone that disturbingly resembled a huge alien vulva.

Level three didn't have a big end-of-level boss, because the whole level was a fight against a massive alien battleship flying serenely through a cramped cavern. Weapon choice, and effective use of the detachable 'Force' device were far more important now, as the environment joined the familiar hazards of bullets and kamikaze enemy ships, and memorisation of the entire level became as critical as accurate shooting.

R-Type has aged really well, retaining both its classic status and unrivalled challenging gameplay, despite the countless clones and imitations that have appeared over the years. Official ports and conversions have been released on the vast majority of consoles, as well as for PC and mobile devices. I bought the mobile-phone version on the day it was released, and I still play both R-Type and R-Type II on my phone, where the relative-touch control method is surprisingly enjoyable.

A bugged mobile update of R-Type II accidentally gave the player ship complete invulnerability until they patched it sometime later, so the online high-scores on Game Centre were not entirely representative of the game's crazy difficulty level.

Chapter 6

Failure is always an option
'They're coming outta the goddamn walls!'

I avoided employment until halfway through 1985, when I applied for a job in the telesales department of a local newspaper group. I had no relevant experience but I thought my two years on a computer studies course had given me decent enough typing skills to compensate for my total lack of everything else. I was interviewed by the manager of the department and the telesales team leader. The manager was Mike, a clean-cut bloke with a formal demeanour and a bemused attitude towards my unlikely application to join his telephone sales team. The leader of the team was a gorgeous ash-blonde called Jayne, which meant I didn't pay any attention to Mike's polite but unsubtle hints of discouragement. He told me what the job involved, more a warning than a sharing of information, while I sat there smiling at Jayne.

They took me into the telesales office, where four young women were working efficiently and without pause on their typewriters and phones, and they sat me at a desk with a typewriter and a telephone headset. Mike told me he was going to phone me and I had to type the details of an advert he wanted to place in one of the local papers. I hadn't used a typewriter for years, and it was nothing like typing on a computer keyboard.

I blundered erratically through the whole process, trying to sound professional on the phone while two-finger typing a vague version of Mike's fake customer details and his hurriedly recited advert to sell a car, or possibly a cat. When it was all over, I went back into Mike's office and sat staring at Jayne while I waited patiently for Mike to get to the part where I was absolutely not at all suited to being a telesales girl. Instead, he asked me if I could start next Monday.

It began badly and it got worse in a hurry. The induction day at a training centre near Worcester was full of enthusiastic journalism graduates and constantly grinning newbies who got extremely excited when we were all asked to talk about our favourite TV advert and why we liked it. When it was my turn, I said I didn't have a favourite advert. I backed up this wildly unpopular claim by saying I didn't like adverts because they interrupted programmes I actually wanted to be watching on TV. I started having post-traumatic flashbacks to the bullshit of art college, caring more about retaining a few scraps of my own self-respect than making any new friends. It wasn't as if I was ever going to be seeing any of the other people on the induction course again, once I was in the telesales office.

Unsurprisingly, I was not very good at being a telesales girl. My typing was substandard and too slow. Every day, we had two deadlines when advert copy was collected from the office to be taken in a van to the printers. If we didn't have time to correct the top copy (Tipp-Ex and overtyping), we had to phone the corrected advert details through to the printers. All of this was happening while new calls were coming through. There was no lull, just a constant, frantic losing battle. For me, anyway. The four young women just got on and dealt with it. I was monumentally out of my depth and I didn't enjoy it at all.

Lunchtime was rigidly enforced, and not the way you might think if you work in an office where everyone stoically works through their lunch break and stays late every day to 'go the extra mile'. Our lunch breaks in telesales were enforced because if we didn't physically leave the office we honestly *could not* stop working. I was sent out every day at lunch time, shaking and sweating, to get some food, to breathe some fresh Hereford air, to calm down and not break under the constant, chaotic pressure.

Jayne tried to encourage me. She told me it would get easier. She said she liked me and could see I wanted to do a good job. Her second-in-command told me I was letting everyone else down and it was more than her job was worth to have me working in their department. Her name was Ann. I didn't like her.

One day, after work, I had to go to a video shop to pick up a rental copy of The Last Starfighter before heading to the car park, a quarter of a mile away from the newspaper office. Ann chose that day to attempt some kind of 'pretending to care' chat when we left the office in the evening. I said I had to go and get a video from the shop, which was in the opposite direction to where she was heading. She didn't believe me. The next day, I had to prove I'd watched the video I told her I was renting because she was convinced I'd lied about it to avoid walking to the car park with her.

After the first month, I was deemed competent enough to join the rota for Saturday mornings. One weekend in four, I'd go into the office on my own and make calls to people who had placed 'For Sale' adverts which had expired. I'd phone them and ask them if they'd sold their bike, or their cooker, or their Persian cat. If they hadn't sold it, they started to get excited because I sounded like a potential buyer, and then I'd ask if they wanted to repeat the advert in the paper. That was usually the point where they'd tell me the first advert was a waste of money and no, thanks very much, but they didn't want to waste any more. Or they'd just swear and hang up. It was nowhere near as fun and rewarding a way to spend a Saturday morning as it sounds.

Somewhere in the middle of my three-month probation period on the telesales team, I bought a truly excellent Spectrum game called The Way of the Exploding Fist. I got it from WHSmith in Hereford during a lunch break. It was an interesting game because it was much more realistic than an arcade action game. It had a serious atmosphere and a sense that it was a proper fighting simulation, with points scored in a similar manner to a real-world karate match, nothing unrealistic or cartoony about the action, and no decapitations or showers of blood. It was tough, but it could be overcome with practice and, as I figured out, by repeated use of a lunging kick-to-the-nads move that was almost always successful if you managed to get the timing spot-on.

The purpose of the three-month probation period was to determine whether someone with no previous relevant experience had any more than a cat-in-hell's chance of meeting the requirements to be a full-time, permanent member of the telesales team. I had been screwing up on a daily basis, often multiple times in one day, with failures ranging from the regular instances of 'loads of typos and a pile of late copy' to inserting my own home telephone number into a small-business advert for lawn replacement.

At the end of the third month I went into Mike's office, fully prepared for the predictable news that he thought I wasn't good enough, and didn't want to keep me on. I wasn't at all prepared for the unexpected news that he thought I had improved noticeably since I started, admired my tenacity in an unfamiliar and challenging role, and wanted to extend my probation period by a month to give me the opportunity to prove I was able to reach the acceptable levels of accuracy and productivity he was sure I was capable of achieving.

I spent the next month doing everything I could to hit Mike's target of being good enough to do the job. I got better at typing. I didn't have to phone late adverts through to the printer after every deadline, just some of them. I took on a few regular business adverts, on top of handling incoming phone calls. I worked hard, really hard, at being good enough, essentially breaking my neck every day to hit a level of mediocrity that felt constantly unattainable.

I didn't have the natural ability to do the job, but I did it anyway, and almost every day of that fourth month I went home exhausted, collapsed on the sofa, and fell asleep. Most days, I didn't have the energy or the enthusiasm to switch my Spectrum on, all I wanted to do was sleep.

I didn't quit, but I was only fooling myself. The rest of the team worked hard but it wasn't breaking them into pieces every day. They could do the job because they had the necessary abilities. It was relentlessly hard for me because I was no good at it, and I was proving it every day by battling in vain to hit the required target of 'average'. But, as the Unknown Soldier song goes, I kept struggling on.

At the end of the fourth month, I went back into Mike's office, not even knowing what I hoped or expected to hear. He told me he was really pleased with the way I'd applied myself to the job. He told me even Ann was pleased with me. He said he had really not been sure at the end of the third month that I was going to stick at it, and he was genuinely impressed that I hadn't given up. He told me he was willing to sign off my probation period and offer me a permanent job on the telesales team.

I thought about what he was saying, and what would happen if I smiled, shook his hand and said thanks. I'd worked myself to exhaustion every day to reach a level deemed satisfactory. I knew I couldn't keep it up for another month, let alone the foreseeable future of my working life. I didn't enjoy the job at all, and I suspect I'd only managed what I had achieved in that fourth month because I had been constantly looking toward the last day as an end to the tiredness and the constant struggling.

I shook Mike's hand and I said thanks, but I didn't smile. I told him I didn't think I could do it, that being 'good enough' was too difficult. He asked me if I understood I'd be turning down the job by saying that, giving me the chance to change my mind. I said yes, I did understand, and that was it.

Mike had a cute assistant called Debbie who helped out on the telesales team and was ridiculously good at everything she did. I told her I was leaving and she asked me why. I said I couldn't do what they did in telesales because I wasn't any good at it. She asked me what I was going to do after I left and I said I didn't know. I asked if she'd go out for a farewell drink with me in her lunch hour and she said yes.

There was a wine bar up the street from the newspaper office so we went there and sat talking for an hour. In four months, I hadn't really had time to talk informally to anyone from the office because we'd all been constantly busy and we took staggered lunch hours to cover the phones. It was the first time in four months that I'd felt relaxed. It had been a mistake to apply for the telesales job, but doing it had taught me a very valuable life lesson: I wasn't invincible, I wasn't good at everything, and I didn't want another job where I'd be constantly knackered.

1985 was a pivotal year for video games. Looking back

now, it's mind-blowing to see the sheer quantity of classic, inspirational games that came out that year. If it had only been Commando, Ghosts 'n Goblins and Gauntlet in the arcades, that would have been more than enough. But there was also Gradius, Paperboy and Space Harrier, and numerous other memorable titles.

Console games released that year included Super Mario Bros on the NES, arguably the most significant and influential game ever released on a console. There was already an indication that games on home computers were developing in different directions compared to their arcade and console counterparts, with titles such as Ultima IV, Tau Ceti, King's Quest II, and The Oregon Trail appearing in 1985. Three years since its release, Spectrum developers were producing ever more polished and technically astounding games, and a whole lot of sequels. In addition to The Way of the Exploding Fist, we had Monty on the Run, Doomdark's Revenge (sequel to The Lords of Midnight), Alien 8, Roller Coaster, and Saboteur.

Four months on probation in telesales hadn't been the most lucrative time of my life but I was able to buy enough Spectrum games to get me through a few months of unemployment while I tried to figure out what I was going to do for my first proper job.

A young woman working at the job centre in Monmouth told me I should apply to join the Civil Service if I wanted to work with computers. I was initially sceptical. I knew all about the Civil Service; it was the place where James Bond worked, run by a bunch of Masons who'd all been to the same private school. I had no chance of getting in there, did I? She told me it wasn't quite like that, but there would be an entrance test and an interview, and I needed two A-levels to apply to be an Executive Officer, which was the grade I'd need to be if I wanted to do computer programming. I'd failed A-level English twice, and barely scraped a pass grade in Geography when I took the exam the second time, but by some unfeasible aberration of the educational rating system of the mid-eighties, my BTEC qualification in computer studies was rated as the equivalent of an A-level pass, or possibly two. It meant I was over the first obstacle, so at the start of 1986 I applied to the Civil Service for an Executive Officer grade computer programming role.

The process for joining the Civil Service dragged on from February to September of 1986, controlled and coordinated with a dehumanizing sequence of commands and instructions that dropped through my letterbox on an irregular basis, and without warning, separated by weeks of hearing nothing at all.

The first letter told me I had to be at an unremarkable grey building somewhere in Wales, at a particular time on a particular date, to take an initial evaluation test. There was no opportunity offered to reschedule the test, or to discuss any aspect of it with anyone from the Civil Service. I found the location on a map, and I drove there on the specified day, arriving about an hour before the specified time because I hadn't wanted to get there late and I had no idea how lost I was going to get on the way there, or how bad the traffic would be.

The building looked like an abandoned school, the test room a featureless space with fifty desks arranged in ten precisely ordered rows. There were already a few people in there when I walked in early, after sitting in my car for forty minutes waiting until what seemed an appropriate time to make my entrance. I didn't speak to anyone else and I didn't see any of the other test candidates talking. One of the test overseers showed me a desk and I sat at it. There was a test paper face down on the desk, a few lines of unambiguous text telling me not to turn it over until instructed to do so. Beside the test paper was a pencil.

The minutes ticked by and the room filled up. At the exact time specified in the letter I'd received, one of the test overseers told us how long we had to complete the test, drew our attention to a clock on the wall, and told us to turn over the test and begin. Thirty seconds later, a bloke stood up to loudly complain about the unfair discrepancy between the task and the time allocated to complete it, before stomping out of the room.

I worked through the test questions, of which there were definitely way too many for anyone to be able to complete all of them in the available time, answering the ones that looked quick and easy while skipping past anything that looked like it was going to take ages to figure out. When the time was up, I'd answered about half the questions and I felt like I'd probably got most of them right.

A month later, a letter arrived telling me to be at a generic office block in London, at a particular time on a particular date, to take a computer programming aptitude test. I went to London on a train, took a tube from Paddington and walked the rest of the way, constantly checking my A-to-Z guide until I reached the building where the aptitude test was being held.

It was much harder than the first test, long questions about averages and ratios and percentages, some questions so convoluted I couldn't even figure out what they were asking, let alone what I was supposed to be answering. My estimate for how many answers I had right was in the twenty percent range, and that felt decidedly optimistic.

I went home and waited, nothing else I could do. A month later, they sent me a letter telling me where and when I had to attend an interview. It was somewhere else in Wales, another generic office building, another specific date and time with no option to request an alternative.

The interview consisted of me sitting on one side of a long wooden table, opposite three people facing me on the other side of it. Two men and one woman. I thought one of the men looked like he might have been in the RAF, based on the style of his moustache. They asked me a bunch of questions, not the sort of questions I would previously have imagined to be included in a Civil Service interview.

For example, they asked me my opinion of Live Aid, which had been really big news the previous year. I'm an idiot, but I'm not stupid. It was obvious, even to me, that anyone who responded to this prompt with "Music is the only way to change the world" or "I was there and I got bladdered, mate" or even "Geldof for pope, let's stick it to the man" would not be getting any more letters from the Civil Service. I went with a middle-of-the-road, impassive assessment, demonstrating that I understood the motivation of the organizers and contributors, appreciated the logistics involved in coordinating such a massive global event, but ultimately believed the long-term solution to famine and genocide in third-world countries was not necessarily a bunch of pop stars trying to bolster their careers with profane public declarations about how much they cared. I was thanked for my time, and I went home.

A month later I opened another letter from the Civil Service. This one told me where I was going to be working and when I was due to start. I've got a feeling I could actually get into trouble for mentioning the department where I worked, not because it dealt with anything particularly sensitive but because mentioning it in the context of an autobiography about video games and generally silly behaviour might breach some agreement I may or may not remember signing when I joined. Let's just say it was a non-profit-making insurance department, and I worked at two different locations in Cardiff between 1986 and 1989.

Inspired by impending full-time employment, I blew most of my remaining telesales earnings on an Atari 520 ST, a 16-bit computer that had been released a year earlier in the summer of 1985. It was a real next-gen evolution, with a proper keyboard, a mouse, and a slot in the side for floppy disks. I kept the Spectrum but I hardly ever used it after getting the Atari ST. The massive improvements in sound and graphics truly put the Spectrum in the shade, and there were loads of games for the ST, quite a few of them extremely entertaining.

Gunship was a helicopter simulator where you flew an Apache gunship on various missions, earned rank promotions and won medals as you progressed through the game. The player character could be permanently killed, or sometimes rendered MIA if you crash-landed behind enemy lines. Either of these occurrences sent the character to an archive list where you could see what rank they had reached and how many medals they had been awarded in their career. It was a single-player game but I often played it with Sadboy in a coffee-fuelled co-op mode where I did the flying while he operated the weapons. We had a packed roster of dead and MIA pilots, all called Chuck in honour of the Missing in Action movie from a year earlier. After watching that film, and Rambo, and the general surge in popularity of other 'Nam-based action films, Gunship was even more of a blast to play. We would deliberately try to take lots of damage from enemy fire, before limping back to a friendly base, in an attempt to earn a Purple Heart medal, but those reckless flights more often ended with yet another Chuck added to the list of fallen and missing heroes.

Xenon was a vertically scrolling shooter with memorable metallic-looking graphics and a definite victory of style over gameplay, the Bitmap Brothers doing everything they could to promote themselves as the ultracool rock stars of video game development. They achieved this goal with Speedball, a violent, futuristic sport played in a slightly tilted top-down view. Containing elements of American football, ice hockey, pinball, and paying homage to (as opposed to blatantly plagiarising) the Rollerball movie, Speedball was a unique and fairly original gaming experience. It was only surpassed by the outstanding sequel, Speedball 2 - Brutal Deluxe.

The sequel to Xenon, Xenon 2: Megablast, was a much better game than the original. There was more going on, the action was far more frantic, and it was just much more fun. I played it a lot, and if I was compiling top-ten lists for each gaming platform (please don't just skip to chapter 17), Xenon 2 would be in my top ten for the Atari ST.

Oids was a must-play for any Asteroids fan, or any Gravitar, Lunar Rescue, or Lunar Lander fan, maybe even any Defender fan, although that last one is a bit of a stretch. It was the first game I'd owned which had a built-in editor for creating your own levels.

Dungeon Master innocently shambled onto the gaming scene with no clue whatsoever as to the monumental impact it would have on video gaming, or the jaw-dropping extent of its legacy. It was a pseudo-3D role-playing game set in a predominantly grey world of flick-screen tunnels and dead-ends. Would RPGs have evolved the way they did without it? Possibly. Would Wolfenstein 3D have existed if Dungeon Master hadn't done what it did? Probably. Would Doom have been Doom without Dungeon Master? More than likely. But still, when you run your finger down a chronological list of first-person computer games, specifically RPGs, Dungeon Master was there first. It pioneered and popularised the way player inventory items were managed, which more than made up for the frustration that came from not having an in-game map. It blended party-based exploration with real-time action, and it sold more copies on the Atari ST than any other game. For a long time, role-playing computer gamers couldn't have been happier.

The Civil Service department I joined ran a six-week introductory training course for computer programming recruits. There were a dozen people in my group, all keen and eager to learn. Only one person struggled hard and eventually quit before the end of the six weeks of training, a bloke called Terry Cope, who we rather uncharitably referred to as Terry Can't Cope when it became evident he wasn't going to be sticking with a career in programming.

Our computer access was on green-screen mainframe terminals, not terminal emulators but actual terminals. This sounds prehistoric to me now, thirty-three years on, knowing that in my own lifetime we've come from an era when there were pretty much no computers at all, at least as far as the majority of the world's population was concerned, to a point where most of us in the first world can't get through five minutes, let alone an entire day, without interacting with some kind of computerised device. I was there when they had mainframe terminals, no email, no external access, no remote working, and I was there to see the last few weeks when there were ashtrays on desks and quite a few people smoked inside the office.

The open-plan training room was in a ten-storey office tower within a medium-security compound near Llanishen. The site was also used by a few other departments, including an RAF driving school. It was the kind of place where security guards patrolled the corridors, randomly checking ID cards and sending dire, official reports to your manager if they caught you walking to the canteen without your ID card on display. It only happened once to me, and once was definitely enough. While the possibility of being dragged outside and shot wasn't actually stated or even implied, it was never formally denied.

The other site, where most of the business teams worked, was a few miles away in the far more salubrious Cathays Park area of Cardiff, in a large, five-storey office building shared with the Welsh Office. It was very different from the Cold War aesthetic style of the Llanishen site, with a far more relaxed atmosphere. I say relaxed, what I mean is it felt like a Club 18-30 holiday resort.

Our department was 'non-profit-making' and we went above and beyond all expectations to maximise the amount of non-profit we achieved. There was a morning break, when everyone trooped down to the canteen for breakfast, a similar afternoon break for tea and coffee, in addition to the hour-long lunch break. There were no shareholders to impress, no sales targets to reach, and no high-performing culture incentivisations going forwards in the insurance space. If you didn't scream in horror, or even cringe at that last sentence, you've either never worked in an office or you're already beyond help.

Of course, it was still the Civil Service so we had our ample share of charisma-bypass drones in suits, doing everything they could to police the fun out of everything on a daily basis. Brian Winterbourne was the archetypal office zombie, the poster boy for fawning, boot-licking, grey-suit lifestyle choices. He was a Senior Executive Officer, two rungs of the Civil Service grade ladder above me, and for a while he was my manager's manager, so he was in a position where he could have a direct impact on my life, which was a tragic state of affairs.

We didn't have email, so any information we wanted to send to other people had to be printed, photocopied, and sent out in reusable internal mail envelopes. Winterbourne subscribed to the belief that there was a corporate barrier preventing conversations with people more than a certain number of grades above you. I was allowed to talk to him, according to his rules, but I couldn't talk directly to anyone higher up. As I may have hinted earlier, the man was a bit of a muppet.

On one occasion, I had to send a memo to a bunch of fairly senior people, telling them we'd made a minor change to a policy screen or something, and one of the fairly senior people was Brian. He came to my desk, clutching the memo, shaking his head and grimacing as if he'd found a stash of photographs showing me playing naked Twister with his parents. He placed the memo on my desk and pointed at the alphabetically ordered recipient list printed at the top of the page, his finger hovering over one particular name, a woman who was a couple of grades higher than him, God's sister in Brian's Civil Service office rulebook. He told me I should have put her name at the top of the list. He was genuinely scared she would be so offended by this insult that she would actually emerge from her office and have words with his manager, who would then have words with him, and those words might put my employment at risk.

I waited until he trudged away, shaking his head, gave him a few minutes to bury himself under a mountain of dread at his desk, then I picked up the memo and went up to the next floor to the office where God's sister lived. I knocked on the door, heard her voice telling me to come in, went inside and sat in the chair opposite her desk. I told her who I was and she asked what she could do for me. I showed her the memo, asked if she minded if the recipient list was in alphabetical order.

"Do you think I care about the order of the recipient list?" she asked.

"Brian Winterbourne told me I should have put your name at the top. He said I'd get in trouble for ordering the list alphabetically."

She shook her head, sighed, and briefly closed her eyes. "What a silly man he is," she said. "Would you like me to let him know I'm perfectly happy with an alphabetic recipient list?"

I said thanks, that would be good. I never heard anything more about it from Brian. He could no longer nag me about the order of the recipient list because the word of God's sister was law, and he couldn't tell me the alphabetical order was acceptable because that would involve admitting he was wrong about it in the first place.

We used to have a laugh with the reusable internal mail envelopes, for example sending a few thousand paper clips to someone, with a note inside the envelope suggesting they send it on to someone else. Weeks later, we'd see the same dog-eared envelope being left by the internal post bloke in some random person's in-tray.

Another prank involved the old-style computer mice with balls inside. Some of the managers had PCs, old basic beige things with four-colour screen displays, that they used as terminal emulators and to run the Hitchhiker's Guide to the Galaxy text adventure. You could roll a ball of Blu-tack the same approximate size as a mouse ball and swap it in a manager's mouse, then just wait and watch what happened when they tried to move the mouse. This kind of stupidity was on a par with sellotaping the receiver button down on a desk phone so it kept ringing after the handset was picked up.

I figured out that I could call a fax machine from my phone, then forward the call to someone else so when they answered their phone they heard the fax machine screeching at them as it tried to make a connection. For a while, this became a very popular office prank in our department, and I took my share of calls from fax machines after making the mistake of telling a few people how to do it.

The canteen in the Cathays Park building had Starforce, a vertically scrolling space shooter, followed by Trojan, a side-scrolling beat-em-up. Both were in vertical arcade cabinets. I was better at Starforce than I ever was at Trojan, but I dropped plenty of 10p coins into both machines. It was the only place I've ever worked where there were video game cabinets in the canteen, but it was also the only place I've ever worked where two of my co-workers sent a birthday card to a young woman in another department, signed it as if I had sent it, and didn't tell me about it for ages.

One of those co-workers on my programming team was Steve Hole. We had a lot of free time between projects because they wanted us to be available during the testing phases in case we had to fix anything the testers found. That might sound crazy, but it was a non-profit-making department so it didn't matter if we weren't coding flat-out every working hour of the day. During these slack periods, Steve and I wrote games in COBOL on the mainframe. It wasn't an optimal platform or programming language for game development, but that was all part of the fun. I wrote a Hangman program which picked random entries from a text file of film titles and also had the option to manually input a word or phrase for two-player gaming. The gallows and hanging man were displayed on the screen in various ASCII characters using CICS output commands.

After that, I wrote a fruit machine program that simulated the spinning reels by rapidly changing a row of four characters using a looping CICS screen output command. I'd been testing it with Steve for about half an hour when the phone on my desk rang. It was one of the mainframe support operators, asking me what FRUITO1 was, because it was performing an unacceptably high volume of screen I/O commands. After that, we learned to give the game programs names that looked like legitimate claims or policy screens. Steve created a Monopoly game and something loosely based on Cluedo. On our next project, I used a version of the code from my Hangman program in a routine for checking customer names. I was learning as much about programming from the games I was writing as from the real work I was supposed to be doing.

Sharing the building with the Welsh Office meant we'd occasionally be evacuated and have to stand outside for a few hours because Plaid Cymru or some other disgruntled bunch of rebels had threatened to blow us all up. A couple of times, protesters climbed on the roof to wave banners while we were evacuated until they got bored and came down.

While I was working in Cardiff I lived in a tiny flat, with a single room where the bed folded into the wall. The first year I was living there, I couldn't afford to turn the heating on in the winter, and I'd go to sleep wearing two T-shirts, a long-sleeved sweatshirt and a thick jumper, waking up in the morning to find the condensation on the inside of the windows had frozen into a layer of ice. I checked my bank account on New Year's Eve, between 1986 and 1987, and I had four pounds in the bank. That was the closest I ever came to being overdrawn.

Aliens was in the cinema in 1986, around the time I started working for the Civil Service. It was the best film I'd ever seen, even better than The Terminator, and it had an eight-week run in the ABC cinema in Hereford. I went to see it four times, three times with various different friends and once on my own. I don't know how many times I've watched the director's cut since then, the version with the Hadley's Hope prologue sequence and a bunch of other restored footage, but I can still name all the colonial marines without cheating, even Frost, Crowe and Ferro, the ones nobody usually remembers.

Aliens was going to be a massive influence on the evolution of video games, particularly after Doom appeared. I'd say it was more of an influence than any film before or since, and I'm not just talking about the licensed games based on the Alien and Predator franchise. The golden age of video game arcades wasn't going to last much longer, but home consoles and PC gaming were about to go completely crazy.

Chapter 7
Knee deep in the dead
'Shots do not hurt other players…yet.'

Two years after joining the Civil Service I was earning enough to be able to turn the heating on in my flat, and I saved up enough money to buy a second-hand KTM motocross bike, a Bell helmet and a pair of Sidi boots. The bike and the helmet were both white, the boots were pink.

My friend Andy got me into motocross, although I'd been to watch plenty of races with my father when I was a lot younger, back when it was called Scrambling. Andy and I had been friends since primary school, and he had been racing for a few years before I started. I was enthusiastic, loved the smell of two-stroke exhaust and the sonic-boom roar of a forty-bike start line, I read Dirt Bike and the American magazine Motocross Action cover to cover every month, but I was never quick enough to do much more than ride around the tracks and get showered with dirt and rocks by everyone else.

When we were practising, I was more interested in finding lumps in the ground to bounce over than improving my cornering technique, and I definitely didn't take it seriously enough for Andy. He would shake his head and tell me, "You're going to wake up in a strange hospital with your leg up in the air."

We travelled all over the place to Sunday race meetings, spending hours in Andy's old Sherpa van. On one long journey, I got hooked on the track 'Rattlesnakes' by Lloyd Cole and I kept rewinding the cassette to play it over and over. Every time it finished, we'd look at each other and nod, and I'd wind it back and play it again.

We raced at two British championship tracks: Hawkstone Park and Farleigh Castle. The Hawkstone Park day was the muddiest I've ever been. There were lakes of thick brown sludge in the deep dips between jumps, and riders were abandoning their bikes in the cloying mire, leaving them upright with only the handlebars, the top of the tank and the rear mudguard sticking up out of the muck.

I took the entire twenty-minute practice session to complete a single lap and I decided that was enough for one day. People were staggering out of the mud through clouds of exhaust smoke, goggles off, white circles around their eyes and mud everywhere else, looking like pandas retreating on The Somme. I found someone in the pits who had their own high-pressure washer and I asked them to spray me with it to get the worst of the mud off. They were initially reluctant to do it, but I promised I wouldn't sue them if I got hurt. I kept my goggles on, and I'm glad I did.

We went back to Hawkstone Park as spectators in 1990, to watch a round of the 500cc world championship. Belgium was some kind of motocross production line in the late eighties and early nineties, churning out numerous world championship contenders. Britain's Dave Thorpe was a three-time world champion, but he swapped from Honda to Kawasaki in 1990 and he wasn't doing well that year, ending up fifth overall at the end of the championship.

We watched him race at Hawkstone and, although he still looked good on the track, there was definitely something not quite right. After one of the races, we walked through the pit area to look at the bikes and the riders. You could walk right past most of them, and it was great seeing world championship contenders up close, mechanics fiddling about with freshly cleaned factory bikes we knew were a hundred times more expensive than the lookalike bikes we saw every Sunday.

We found Dave Thorpe's trailer and joined the big crowd gathered around it, dozens of fans, riders from support races, Hells Angels, all barely moving, totally silent, one of those weirdly poignant real-life moments I can never think about without getting goosebumps. Thorpe was out in front of his trailer, sitting in an old deck chair, holding a mug in one hand and just looking at nothing, a proper thousand-yard stare. His boots were off and I remember looking at his filthy socks, worn and ripped, and I wondered if they were the ones he was wearing when he'd won the championship in 1989. He wasn't doing anything, just sitting there, hardly moving, maybe thinking about the race he'd just finished, maybe regretting his decision to change to Kawasaki.

It was so quiet; nobody in the crowd was talking, nobody was going up to him and asking for his autograph, we were all just standing there looking at him as if he was a peerless warrior back from some distant conflict. I thought he looked ancient, powered up with a lifetime of racing knowledge, experience and hard-won victories, but he was only a year older than me, twenty-eight years old in 1990.

I never had a motocross game on the Atari ST, but there were tons of other games, more new ones coming out every week. I wanted to sell some of the older games I no longer played, so I put an advert in a local Herefordshire paper, using the same telesales department where I'd worked a few years before.

I answered the phone the day the advert had appeared in the paper, and I started talking to a bloke who sounded interested in the games I had for sale. He told me he didn't want to buy the games but I should go to his house and take them with me, and he'd sort me out with some new games. He turned out to be someone who worked in British Telecom with my friend Johnny Butt, and they called him Dippy Mitchell because he was infamously daft.

I went to Dippy's house on an old estate on the western outskirts of Hereford, lugging a dozen boxed Atari ST games in a couple of carrier bags. I had a different car by then, a VW Polo, because the Lada wouldn't have coped with regularly being driven to Cardiff, and I was spending the majority of weekends at my parents' house, mostly so I could go to the pub and the cinema with my friends.

Dippy had a 'Blitz' device plugged into his Atari ST, with software to circumvent the protection on game disks which otherwise couldn't have been copied using the computer's standard disk-copy program. He demonstrated how it worked by copying one of the games I had with me, then playing the game from the copied disk. He showed me a couple of disk boxes, both full of floppy disks, probably a hundred of them, all copies of Atari ST games. He asked me if I wanted copies of any of them. I didn't want to appear greedy, and we had to come to an arrangement about the supply and demand of blank floppies because I hadn't brought any with me, so I only took a few copied games during that first visit.

One of those games was a film tie-in based on the Predator movie that had come out in 1987. I saw Predator at the cinema in Hereford with a group of my friends on a weekend I was back home from Cardiff. I always thought of it as being 'back home' because I didn't like the tiny flat in Cardiff and I didn't want to think of it as my home, just a place I stayed during the week while I was at work. I was paying off the mortgage and paying all the bills associated with 'a home' but I didn't want to be there any longer than absolutely necessary. I wasn't massively impressed by Predator at the time. I didn't think it was better than The Terminator and it was certainly not in the same league as Aliens, but it had Arnie and a bunch of other fairly cool characters, and there was plenty of action and numerous quotable lines.

The Atari ST Predator game was a side-scroller where you

ran through a jungle trying not to die every five seconds. It looked quite good, and the frequent 'Predator vision' sequences where you had to avoid the Predator's triangular target were well done, but it was a hard game and it felt quite slow and repetitive. I probably would have played it a lot more if I'd paid for it.

Between 1986 and 1989, I saw and played several games in work on managers' IBM PCs. They were bringing the games in on floppy disks and installing them on their work PCs. There didn't seem to be any rules to prevent this, or any fear of introducing a virus, let alone any concept of IT security.

There was no network linking the PCs to each other, or to any kind of Windows server. The PCs ran mainframe emulator software, and they were connected to the mainframe and a local printer, but that was the full extent of the network. More than one of the managers had the Hitchhiker's Guide to the Galaxy text adventure installed. One of them had Elite, the original version with four-colour CGA graphics, another had Tetris.

My favourite out of all the old PC games, which must have been loaded on all the available PCs in the department, was another four-colour CGA game: Alley Cat. It was a bizarre arcade cat-sim where you played as the titular Alley Cat and you had to jump up on rubbish bins in a back alley, then onto a fence, and then jump or bounce your way in through windows to enter various cat-themed mini games. One mini game involved catching mice that appeared in a giant wedge of cheese, and there was one where you had to jump up a series of horizontal platforms made of hearts to reach another cat, where you could produce more and more kittens if you progressed far enough through the game. Like a lot of platform games from that era, it was a frantic, spasm-inducing button masher, but it was also ridiculously addictive. The severely limited colour palette (most things were pink, and the cat was black) and 'broken Stylophone' music only added to the game's simplistic charm.

Halfway through 1989, we started to hear rumours that our Civil Service department was going to be privatised and significantly shrunk, with half the staff either being made redundant or relocated to London. They were only rumours, and nothing had officially been announced, but I decided to get out while getting out was still a choice. I started looking for mainframe programming jobs and I was offered an analyst/programmer position at an independent insurance company in Gloucester, with a start date in December 1989.

The last manager I worked for in the Civil Service was an efficient but friendly Welsh woman called Eirian. A week before my final day working there, she told me the leaving collection for me was quite a considerable amount and she wanted to know if there was anything specific I'd like as a leaving present. I told her I'd like something I could keep with me to remind me of my time with the Civil Service and all the good friends I had made there. I gave it some thought for a few seconds before telling her I'd like a pen. She appeared momentarily flustered, asking me if I was sure, because the collection was a serious amount of money. I said yes, please buy a pen with as much of the collection as possible, and spend the remainder on a card.

On my last day, we had the obligatory office leaving-speech pantomime, with the entire department gathered around. Somewhere between fifty and sixty people were listening as Eirian thanked me for all my hard work, cracked a couple of tame in-jokes referencing some of my less-impressive moments as a junior programmer, and wished me all the very best in my new job on the wrong side of the border. She gave the leaving gift an impressive build-up, then she handed me a large envelope containing the card, and an exquisitely wrapped but comparatively tiny rectangular present. It doesn't matter how expensive a pen is, the box is always going to be small. I knew this when I asked for the pen. I'm guessing everyone knows this.

I took the present, stared in feigned disbelief at the small box in my hand, looked up at Eirian and said, loudly enough for everyone to hear, "Is that it?"

Eirian glared at me, called me a bastard, and started laughing. She gave me a hug, asked if I had done it on purpose, and looked suitably unconvinced when I said I just liked pens.

A week later, I started work at the insurance company in Gloucester. It was a thirty-mile drive, and they didn't have a staff car park, so I had to park on the side of the road near the office, which meant I had to arrive more than an hour before the building opened otherwise all the roadside spaces would be taken.

The city centre was only a few hundred yards from the office, and I walked to the shops every lunch hour to check out the latest games and consoles. I still had the Atari ST but I bought a Sega Mega Drive early in 1990. I had Sonic on the Mega Drive, but I hadn't been as impressed by it, or as hooked on it, as I had expected. There were other Mega Drive games I preferred, some of the shooters like Thunder Force IV, and more traditional platformers like Castle of Illusion.

I'd been in my new job with the Gloucester insurance company for four months when I fulfilled Andy's motocross prediction and woke up in a strange hospital with my leg up in the air. We went down to Wells, near Taunton, on Sunday the first of April, 1990, to race at an ACU motocross meeting. There hadn't been any rain for weeks, just a run of hot, dry days that left the Wells hillside track a parched, cracked patchwork of hard-baked mud, unforgiving as concrete.

I'd recently part-exchanged my KTM 125 for a Suzuki 250, and it was the first race where I'd used the new bike. Smiley and Sadboy drove down to watch the racing with Andy's brother, Grant. After the practice session, Grant told me I should be getting more air-time over the big jump where a large crowd was watching. I thought he was right; I'd been popping over it but not achieving any spectacular height or distance.

I went out for the first race and joined the queue waiting to ride out to the start line. Different race organisers had different methods of ordering the start line. They couldn't let everyone choose their own place or there'd be a dozen riders fighting over the best race-line to the first corner. At the Wells track, they had a bucket full of wooden pegs. Each peg had a number written on it in black felt pen. I reached into the bucket and took out a peg with the number thirteen on it. Number thirteen, on April Fool's day. And I'm not making this up. Ten years later, while I was watching the first Final Destination film, I realised I should have handed the peg back, turned my bike around, and pushed it slowly and carefully back to the pits. Instead, I rode out following the bloke who'd picked the number twelve peg and took my place thirteenth on the start line.

They had one of those metal gates where each of the places on the line has a separate eighteen-inch horizontal metal bar that drops when the race starts. They hold up a sign-board with the number thirty on it when there's thirty seconds before the start, then they hold up a board with the number ten on it. After that, the gate could drop at any time within the next ten seconds.

The first corner at the Wells track was the same as the first corner at every other motocross track on the planet, it was total carnage. As well as being the title of the sequel to Smash TV, total carnage is not something to recklessly hurl yourself into on a motocross track, not unless you're one of the riders who has the ability and the intention to finish in a top-ten position. I was excluded on both counts, so I trailed along with the back of the pack, picking my way through the dust cloud past the fallers and their downed bikes. The ones who had made it through unscathed were far ahead, tearing away from the shambles and the stragglers. I hadn't gone to Wells to win, or even finish in the top half, but there was always a good scrap going on at the back, another muppet or two like me, with the bike and the gear and a friend with a van, but who were really only there for the joy of riding and the intoxicating smell of two-stroke exhaust fumes.

I went over the big jump cautiously on the first lap, spending the minimum amount of time airborne. The ruts on the far side of the jump were deep, criss-crossed gouges of serrated, rock-hard, sun-baked mud. If you didn't completely clear the ruts, you had to stick with the one you landed in, or risk getting pitched off sideways. I could have got more airtime, I kept telling myself all around the next lap. It would even be safer than taking the jump at a sedate pace, because I'd land on the other side of the dangerous ruts.

I was still considering how fast I needed to be going as I approached the jump, not fully committed even when I was on the face of the ramp. I made the wrong decision, and I made it too late, twisting the throttle back at the moment the front wheel cleared the lip of the ramp. I don't know exactly what happened, because it was all over so quickly, but the sudden acceleration flipped the bike backwards as it left the jump.

There's a gap in my memories, between being on the bike as I hit the face of the jump and half-rolling, half-staggering to the side of the track, away from the bikes landing behind me, the race leaders who had caught up and overtaken me while I was lying on the rutted track in front of the jump.

People in the crowd were leaning over the safety rope a yard behind the fence, calling out to me, asking If I was okay. I waited for a lull between the thunder of landing bikes, grabbed the bars of my Suzuki and hauled it upright. A track marshal waved at me, asking something about my knee. I shook my head, swung my right leg over the saddle and flipped out the kickstart lever. My right leg felt fine. I started the bike and rode away, changing up through the gears with my left foot, feeling a rough, grinding sensation inside my boot. I told myself I must have got a stone in there, maybe a few chunks of gravel, because that's what it felt like.

I rode all the way around the track, no longer enthusiastic or enjoying what I was doing. I rode up the face of the jump and guided the front wheel carefully through a wide, deep rut when I landed. I went around the track for another three or four laps and felt a hopeless surge of relief when the black and white chequered flag went up, telling me I could quit now. There was relief, but there was also a fear I wasn't acknowledging.

Going back to the van in the pits meant I had to get off the bike. Getting off meant standing up, putting weight on my left foot. I hobbled to the St John's Ambulance tent, where I was told it was probably a sprain, but I should get it x-rayed just in case. It was coming up to half past one in the afternoon. We didn't get home until almost nine o'clock that night. I sat in the van for most of the afternoon, limped around the pits in an unhappy daze, and went to the burger van with Smiley, Grant and Sadboy. Grant kept apologising for telling me to get more air-time, but we were all laughing about it. We found one of the warning posters: 'Motorsport is dangerous', and I stood next to it with a fake miserable expression that was not quite as miserable as I felt, while Sadboy took some photos.

The following day, Monday morning, I phoned work and said I wouldn't be in until later because I had to go to hospital to get an x-ray.

It turned out I wouldn't be back in work for six weeks. My left ankle was smashed up pretty badly, so swollen that they couldn't operate on it until Friday that week. When they operated on it, they fixed it up as well as they could, held the bits together with a screw and some wire, and I was stuck with my lower leg in a cast for a couple of weeks.

I did such a good job of recovering, and learning to walk again, that I was told I should have been back in work a week earlier when a manager saw me walking in on my first day back. I learned another valuable life lesson from that: never put yourself out for corporate drones who don't have your interests at heart, and never rush back to work after a serious injury, because it just isn't worth it.

Throughout the nineties, Gloucester had a few independent game shops, as well as the usual chainstores like WHSmith which all had large game departments. One indie game shop became my favourite, a place run by a great character called Dave Fryer.

Dave was a hardcore gamer as well as a game shop owner. He liked the consoles but he was forever mocking me and the other regulars in the shop because we didn't own IBM PCs. He'd have his own PC on the counter in the shop, and he'd show us games like Wing Commander, telling us how he'd be on games like that later while we were at home playing kids' games on our consoles.

The first PC I bought was a 386, with the DOS operating system and Windows 3.11, a shell application invoked from the DOS command line. PC games at that time were also run from the DOS command line, with no real concept of Windows games until the launch of Windows 95, a self-contained operating system running independently of DOS.

My collection of gaming devices was growing. The Spectrum was boxed up in the attic with a pile of games, the Atari ST saw occasional use, but I was mostly buying new games for the Mega Drive and my PC.

When the Super Nintendo came out in the UK in 1992, I bought one straight away. In the shop, Dave had been telling us for ages that it was going to be huge, the next big thing, and he wasn't wrong.

A lot of the SNES games had their names prefixed with 'Super', so there was Super Tennis, Super Castlevania IV, Super R-Type, Super Ghouls 'n Ghosts, bestselling game Super Mario World, and a long list of other 'Super' games as well as plenty without the prefix such as F-Zero, Gradius III, Pilotwings and Altered Beast.

Sadboy was a big fan of Super Tennis. It wasn't licensed or endorsed by any official tennis tournament or governing body, so the characters in the game either had no surnames or were given weird, soundalike names. Boris Becker was represented by a character called Obekka, which Sadboy found truly hilarious. He'd shout the name while dropping the controller in disgust whenever he lost a match, or sometimes while queuing in a Chinese takeaway.

Many SNES games suffered from slowdown and generally poor performance, particularly the early releases. Super R-Type was infamous for its appalling slowdown which rendered it virtually unplayable in several sections where the SNES seemed to be struggling to cope with the demands of the game. Other games, with an equal amount of graphical action, had no obvious issues, which suggested the performance problems were related to inadequate coding and optimisation rather than shortcomings of the hardware.

Super Castlevania IV was a great game, one of my favourites on the SNES, and a candidate for one of my top-five platform games of all time. It was a big game, with long, difficult levels full of aggressive enemies and deadly environmental hazards. I particularly appreciated the horror theme, having been a dedicated fan of the genre ever since I started watching Hammer horror films late at night on TV when I was in my early teens.

Super Castlevania IV crammed in a wide variety of horror classics (I won't call them clichés), from the whip-fodder skeletons and bats at the start of the game to bosses including Frankenstein's monster and Dracula. I completed the game, but it was a tough challenge with some truly exasperating boss fights. There was no way to save the game, and it only gave you a progress password at the end of each level, a system that nowadays would be ridiculed and decried as unfair and cruel. For those of us who had been there since the genuine hardcore days of 'Game Over - back to the start', the password system felt like cheating. Utterly necessary, but still cheating.

There were plenty of games that were exclusive to the SNES, and not just the obvious Nintendo games like anything with Mario in the title. ActRaiser sticks in my memory as both a classic SNES-only title and a truly great game. It was a unique amalgamation of two totally different game types, which really shouldn't have worked out well, and definitely shouldn't have worked out as brilliantly as it did. Half the game was spent building an ever-expanding empire in a top-down city-builder style mode and the other half was spent battling through side-scrolling platform environments to unlock areas for the ongoing empire-building. It was a remarkable game, familiar but in an extremely original way, fun to play, and filled with emotional moments. Nobody else did emotional video games quite like the ones on the SNES.

Skyblazer's downbeat emotional ending has stayed with me since I completed the game back in 1994. It's a decent enough platform action game with a mythical theme, and it ends with a fairly predictable climactic boss battle. After the fight, the sorceress you spent the whole game fighting to rescue is left alone with the old bloke who was your mentor and occasional shopkeeper through the game. The sorceress asks where you've gone, and says she didn't get a chance to reward you for your courage. The old bloke tells her that heroes don't fight for thanks or rewards, and that you've gone off to seek your destiny in adventure. The screen fades to show your character flying off alone over a scrolling Mode-7 landscape towards an unknown fate, not unlike Shane's ambiguous final ride at the end of the classic western, and no less poignant or moving.

I remember how I felt at the time, watching the end credits roll while my pixellated on-screen avatar flew away without the girl or the gold or even a word of thanks. I thought it was sad and perfect, endearingly cinematic, a true masterclass in minimalist storytelling that treated the player as a grown-up who would appreciate the pathos and not rage over the lack of a reward. I must have been tired from playing the game a bit too long in that session, because my eyes started watering as I took out the cartridge and put it back in its box.

Meanwhile, in the alternative universe of PC gaming during the last days of 1993, with hardly any fanfare to accompany a free shareware version of the first chapter, the most important video game in history was about to be released.

I'd played Catacomb Abyss and Wolfenstein 3D, so I thought I knew a thing or two about 3D-shooter games. Dave Fryer stood behind the counter in his shop, waving a three-inch disk at me and shaking his head. "You're going to love this, John. This is going to be the best game you ever play. Trust me." He showed me the label on the disk, one word written there in blue biro: Doom.

Dave wouldn't give me the disk because he only had one, and his PC was at home that day so he couldn't copy it for me. I don't know where he got the disk from. He tended to keep quiet about some of his contacts in the covert underworld of software acquisition. "Why don't you come round my house this evening?" Dave said. "I'll get it loaded by then and you can have a go on it."

Dave was married, with what seemed like a whole house full of kids. I think he had three sons, possibly four. The youngest was about five years old, and they were all really polite, calling me John and asking loads of questions about my computer and console collection.

Dave had his PC booted up when I arrived. The kids had already seen Doom running and they were excited, hyped up and eager to watch me playing it. One of the older ones was complaining that the youngest one was playing up. Dave was ignoring it all, loading Doom while we sat side-by-side in front of his PC. The loading screen showed a buff action-movie bloke in green body armour firing a gun against a mostly red backdrop. Above him, the word Doom was written in towering, angular metallic letters, blue at the top fading into gold at the bottom.

The chapter select only had the option to choose the first chapter, because that was all there was in the shareware version. The chapter was called 'Knee deep in the dead'. Even the name of the chapter was simultaneously ominous and darkly amusing, hinting at the full-scale carnage ahead.

Starting a new game gave you the chance to select a difficulty level. The available options started with two that sounded like they were for crybabies who didn't know what a fire button was for, the hardest one: Ultra-violence, and the one that seemed a good choice to start on: Hurt me plenty.

Nothing could have prepared me for that first go on Doom, because there was nothing like it before it arrived. On a basic level, it sounded similar to Wolfenstein 3D: first person view with guns, but everything about Doom was just bigger and better and more violent and just more everything.

I don't know how long I'd planned to stay in Dave's house playing Doom, but I do know I stayed there a lot longer than that.

We took turns blundering around the first area, firing wildly at the undead soldiers until we ran out of bullets for the pistol or died to the first imp's fireball attack. The game could be saved at any time, and I soon learned to wait until I had a lucky streak of kills and a decent amount of health and armour before saving. I started to memorise the map layout of the first area, the item locations, and all the dark corners where enemies were lurking.

An hour later, I could reach the end of the first area without taking more than a few hits, my pistol ammo maxed out, and a decent amount of armour. The second area was a tougher challenge but it also contained a huge surprise. At the end of a narrow, dead-end corridor there was a window, and through the window we could see a chainsaw on top of a stone pillar in a small, apparently inaccessible room. We had no idea how to get into the room. I found a button in another room, where the floor was toxic green slime, and I pushed the button and found a new area where a section of wall had opened up, but the area didn't lead to the chainsaw room. I went back to the dead-end corridor and gazed longingly through the window at the chainsaw. It was right there, an actual chainsaw in a video game, shiny and yellow, ready and waiting to turn me into Leatherface or, even more exciting, Bruce Campbell's demon-butchering character, Ash, from Evil Dead 2.

We failed to reach the secret room in area two that night, and it wasn't until I'd spent many more hours, days, weeks, playing Doom that I finally (accidentally) shot the right piece of wall to open the passage leading to the chainsaw. Luckily, the chainsaw appeared again in the third area of chapter one, in an easier-to-reach location.

After the pistol, the next firearm to appear was a shotgun. A new enemy, simply called a sergeant, carried this gun and dropped it when he died. Imps went down to a single shotgun blast if you were close enough, and small groups of zombie soldiers could all take damage from the spread of the shot at longer ranges. Tactical weapon-swapping between the pistol and the shotgun was very satisfying, ammo conservation feeling rewarding rather than tedious.

Not long after midnight, when most of Dave's kids had gone to bed, I reluctantly decided it was time I went home. Dave copied the Doom shareware files onto a floppy disk which stayed in my pocket for the forty-five minutes it took me to drive home and boot up my PC.

I installed Doom and spent the next two hours 'checking it was running properly' by battling my way from the start of the game until I got beyond the point I had reached on Dave's PC. I saved the game, told myself I had to quit, killed a couple more demons, saved the game, seriously considered quitting, killed a few more demons, saved the game, promised myself I'd really quit this time, and finally went to bed at about half past three in the morning.

I had Doom dreams that night, no monsters or guns, just a constant rushing journey along tilting, dimly lit corridors, my dream view replicating the restricted perspective in the game. I woke up late, thinking it had been a weirdly realistic dream, turned the PC on and loaded Doom.

Looking back now, with twenty-five years of hindsight and thousands of hours on first-person shooters, Doom's controls were rather awkward. I'm sure they seemed perfectly fine at the time, and the strangeness of the controls is not a prominent memory of my early days with the game. I play first-person games on mouse and keyboard using the standard WASD movement keys, the same as the majority of right-handed gamers. Forward and backward movement is controlled with the W and S keys respectively, and side-to-side movement (strafing) is controlled with the A and D keys. Turning, and looking up and down, is controlled with the mouse. That's the normal setup for FPS games and most other mouse-and-keyboard controlled games involving any kind of movement in a three-dimensional game world.

Doom's original control setup didn't use the mouse. Movement (forward, backward and turning left and right) was controlled with the cursor keys. Strafing involved holding Alt while turning. There were other odd key bindings, and overall it wasn't exactly the most optimal or ergonomic control layout. At the time, knowing nothing of WASD or mouse-aiming, I just got on with it and learned to play Doom with its default key bindings and no mouse.

Original Doom had three chapters: Knee deep in the dead, The shores of hell, and Inferno. The first chapter was wonderful, a moon base overrun by demonic alien bad guys where you could pretend to be in the Aliens movie while tearing through partially cloaked Predator-esque monsters with a chainsaw. Ammo occasionally ran low if you went nuts with the mini-gun, but most of the time you could sprint around in a reckless manner, blasting away and loving every minute of it. The double team of bigger, tougher demons at the end of the chapter posed a minor challenge but they were slow, quite clueless, and they only had the 'green blobby plasma' ranged attack which was easy to dodge.

The shores of hell started to populate levels with more enemies that didn't drop guns or ammo when they died, and Inferno was often a ponderous stop/start slog through huge crowds of the damn things. Recklessly blasting along futuristic corridors was abandoned in favour of a cautious, ammo-conserving crawl through narrow fissures between black rock walls, constantly being ambushed by hordes of floating skulls and blobby tomato demons, neither dropping any ammo.

When my brain hears 'Doom', it recalls images drawn almost exclusively from chapter one. The rest of the game was still good, still worthy of being part of the most significant video game in history, but I personally would have liked more of the game to have made me feel the way chapter one made me feel: a tooled-up action hero living out an Aliens-meets-Evil-Dead-2 monster-splattering fantasy.

One game I almost forgot I'd played in 1993 was Syndicate. In some ways it was ahead of its time, with cyberpunk dudes in long coats six years before The Matrix came out, but from another point of view its ambitious theme was betrayed by its repetitive, often frustrating gameplay.

I didn't know I liked role-playing games before I bought The Elder Scrolls: Arena. It came out in March 1994 and it was insanely ambitious, with claims of a massive open world, hundreds of cities with their own economies, multiple different geographical zones including deserts, swamps and frozen tundra.

The reality was a captivating mix of sword-and-sorcery staples (goblins, war-hammers, dungeons, quests, mages, warriors, thieves, etc.) and smoke-and-mirrors programming creating the feeling that you were travelling around in a huge open world.

The game started in a dungeon cell beneath a city. Depending on your choice of character class, escaping the dungeon was either going to be really, really hard or nightmarishly impossible.

A lot of the things I liked about Arena were changed or completely removed in subsequent Elder Scrolls games. In

Arena, character classes were fixed, with each one having significant advantages and disadvantages, for example the basic warrior and thief classes could never cast spells. Pure magic classes could only wear the weakest of armour, and the Battlemage was arguably capable of becoming the most ridiculously overpowered class in the game. In an attempt to balance this out, disadvantaged classes leveled up quicker but they were never going to be as powerful as some of the slower-leveling classes.

Arena's spell system was brilliant, and it's a real shame they ditched the deeply customisable magic system for the generic spells we ended up with in Skyrim. For example, Arena had a spell that could unlock locked doors and containers. Using the spellmaker, you could create your own version of the spell that had a percentage chance to open a lock, based on your character level. At a low level, say level five, you'd need a spell with at least ten-percent chance per level or it would be too useless to be worth creating. However, at a low level, you wouldn't have enough mana (magic power) to cast the spell, and you probably wouldn't have enough gold to buy the base spell anyway.

Later, much later, when you reached level twenty, creating and casting an unlock spell with a five-percent chance (per level) was dirt cheap, both in terms of the cost of the spell and the mana cost of casting it and, with the simple mathematical result of five-percent chance multiplied by your twenty character levels, you had a spell with a one-hundred percent chance of opening any lock.

The level-twenty spell exploitation could be used with other spells, such as damage reflection, giving you an impenetrable magical barrier that reflected one-hundred percent damage back at your attacker.

Even as an overpowered Battlemage, reaching level twenty was a long, time-consuming journey. I figured out a lazy way of gaining experience, involving sleeping in a house with a specific floorplan where enemies spawned during the night. I was grinding, although I didn't know that term at the time, and I was immensely pleased with myself.

The difference between grinding and farming, because it's vital we clarify these terms, can be summarised like this: 'Grinding' is the repetition of an activity, usually low-risk with zero or negligible immediate reward, and often tedious, in order to reach a long-term goal.

An example of extreme grinding was an achievement-related task in The Lord of the Rings Online which involved killing a ridiculous number of Writhing Death Maggots or some such trash enemy. Due to the sheer quantity that had to be slain, the achievement wasn't going to be gained through natural game progression. You had to go to an area where these things spawned, and you had to get into a kill-wait-kill infinite loop of drudgery for a few hours.

I went to a cave in a level thirty-ish area not far from Rivendell, when I was maxed out at level fifty, and I settled in for a mindless grind on maggots. While I was in there, I joined a conversation in the guild chat channel to let my online guild members know how much fun I wasn't having.

A couple of them perked up and asked where I was grinding these maggots because they needed to complete the incredibly boring chore too.

Soon, there was a team of high-level players in the cave with me, sharing the kills as we tirelessly slaughtered maggot after maggot whenever they spawned. The guild chat channel was filled with epic tales of our slowly rising kill-count, random guild members were entering the cave, witnessing the mind-numbing tedium for themselves, and leaving in disgust.

To add to the stupidity, the cave was a location for a challenging level-thirty quest. We watched as a cautious level-thirty player entered the cave and did whatever they needed to do to summon the terrifying beast that needed to be killed. As soon as it appeared, one of us casually swatted it and it died. The bemused level-thirty player sent us a grateful message in global chat, asked us what we were doing, pretended not to think we were tragic losers, and left the cave. Half an hour later, another keen level-thirty player came into the cave to battle evil, and the tragic pantomime was repeated.

And that is 'Grinding'.

'Farming' is the repetition of an activity, possibly risky, often involving a specific foe or foes, where the goal is to obtain something valuable directly from the target, usually a particular rare item that is known to be sometimes dropped when the enemy is killed.

Farming may actually feel like grinding, but the end goals are distinctly different. If I leveled up from nine to ten by killing a large number of low-level enemies, that would be grinding. If I killed a large number of specific enemies, in an attempt to obtain a unique magic weapon they had a small chance of dropping, that would be farming. A side-effect of farming might be that your character levels up or achieves a trophy for killing a certain number of enemies, but it wouldn't qualify as grinding if the main goal of killing all those enemies was to gain a specific loot drop.

Back in Tamriel, the Arena game was a heck of a lot of fun with just one feature that I absolutely did not like: Riddles. I don't know if the inclusion of the main-quest riddles was a nod to the 'Riddles in the dark' chapter of The Hobbit, but they were just an inconvenient annoyance in Arena.

After battling through each large main-quest dungeon zone, a point would be reached where further progress would not be possible until a riddle was solved. The riddles were not easy, and there was nothing to suggest they were not related to the content of the game, apart from one of them, which was. My progress on the main quest-line was scuppered a third of the way through, until the riddle solutions were published in a PC gaming magazine, but I didn't stop playing the game. There were plenty of places to go, monsters to kill, and legendary items to obtain to keep me playing Arena for many months.

If you want to mock my feeble riddle-solving ability, this was the one I foundered on:

> My second is performed by my first,
> And, it is thought,
> A thief by the mark of the whole
> Might be caught.

No, I'm not telling you the answer. Go and Google it, and remember I didn't have that option back in 1994.

Chapter 8

Musical Interlude Two
'The world could end for all I care.'

While I was at the Gloucester insurance company between 1990 and 1994, I trained after work in the gym at the Kingsholm rugby ground. It was a decent gym, not exclusively monopolised by rugby players, and they'd occasionally hold special events there, such as the time they had Alex Georgijev (Hawk from Gladiators) in there, doing a training seminar. He was a massive bloke; I saw him compete in a Mr Wales competition and they had to put him in a Super-Heavyweight category on his own.

Most Sunday mornings I drove to Hereford and trained with Johnny Butt at Rex Pontin's gym, down by the river, next to the rowing club. Johnny Butt had a key to the gym door because he was one of Rex's trusted regulars. We'd turn up early on Sunday morning and unlock the gym, and we'd get most of our session done before anyone else turned up. Rex's gym was just a big empty space, like a warehouse, with bare brick walls and exposed metal joists. In the winter it was bitterly cold inside and we'd train with our coats on until we warmed up. If people had been walking around inside with wet boots on, or the river had flooded, there would be ice on the floor and sometimes on the benches and the bars.

There was no membership fee, you just turned up and put a pound in a metal box bolted to the wall by the door. Rex would come in, open the box, count the money and start shouting in a cockney accent, "Which one o'you baggas ain't paid?" and we'd all be shaking our heads, saying, "Not me Rex, I put my pound in there. Have you counted it right?"

Johnny Butt was the first person I knew who bought a video camera. It was a big Sony thing, about a foot long. He'd bring it to the gym and we'd make training films, or films of me fighting one of the punch bags while pretending to be drunk, acting out pub-brawl clichés. "Did you spill my pint?" "You heard I can take me." "You're my best mate's pint."

I bought the same type of video camera and I got hooked on filming everything. We'd shoot interview films where one of us would wear a cardboard Elvis mask or a full overhead gorilla mask and we'd just talk complete bollocks, or we'd act out scenes from films, mostly Evil Dead 2, then watch it back by plugging the camera into a TV while we filmed ourselves watching it on the other camera.

One Saturday I was hanging around in a record shop in Hereford and some Welsh bloke I didn't know came up to me, saying, "I saw you in that video, it's you isn't it?" while other people in the shop started staring because this was 1991 and it probably sounded like I was a film star or something. The Welsh bloke was one of Johnny Butt's friends from

Abergavenny. He'd seen some of the Elvis-face interview footage and a few other clips, and he somehow recognised me when he saw me in the shop.

We filmed all sorts of things. Johnny Butt set the camera up in his Ford Capri and filmed himself driving around Hereford at night. We went to an old, derelict graveyard and made a silly horror film 'Car Crash Graveyard Nightmare' using the gorilla mask and an axe I borrowed from my father's garden shed. During the faked axe-murder sequence, Johnny Butt accidentally cut me on the back of my neck with the axe and we filmed him looking at the blood on the axe blade, trying not to laugh while he said, "What have I done? What have I done?".

We'd never seen anything like the kind of home movies we were shooting, everything from a martial arts fight with baseball bats in my back garden to a rubbish bin being blown up with a bomb made from air-bomb repeater fireworks stuffed inside a Coke can.

I decided to record a video diary in 1992, filming myself for a few minutes every day, usually in the evening, while I talked about what had happened that day or just sighed and shook my head at the futility of it all. Sometimes there would be guest diary entry presenters if my friends were visiting me, and the occasional 'on location' diary entry if I was out in the evening and I took the camera with me. I tried not to miss a day, mostly successfully, even on the days when I got home late and didn't feel like doing it. Some of those entries turned out to be the funniest. Most people who've watched any of the video diary footage reckon it's the most depressing thing they've ever seen.

On a return trip from a Motocross race, halfway through 1992, I turned the video camera around and filmed myself while I was holding it, probably inventing selfies but not self-obsessed enough to wonder whether I was the first person to do it, or if I should be thinking up a twee little name for the activity.

It was during the first couple of years of the nineties that Unknown Soldier was reinvented as the Best Worst Band in the World. Sadboy was on vocals, with occasional guest appearances by Smiley, Johnny Butt and Grant. I started playing the guitar on the new songs, and we had a drum machine providing the beat, usually the same beat on every song. In place of the original incarnation's fumbled attempts at serious anarcho-punk, the reborn Unknown Soldier was pure stupidity, churning out a steaming pile of raucous, musically incompetent songs about drinking, driving, failed relationships, bodybuilding, Belgians, memories from school, letting people down, and Parkaman, a notorious Hereford nutjob who wore a filthy parka and shouted profanities as he shambled around the city centre.

From the lost archives of Unknown Soldier, here are the full lyrics to 'Someone Else's Pint', widely acknowledged as the best/worst song we ever recorded:

> I was down at the pub, right out of me mind
> My fourteenth pint I was trying to find
> Best mate Dave, lying on the floor
> D'you want my pint man? Can't take any more

> Up to the bar, I need more swill
> Dear me Charlie, Dave's looking ill
> I got to the bar and I'm in the queue
> It's a pint for me, and a Perrier for you
>
> The pint in me hand, it's getting low
> Whose round is it? I gotta know
> Tennents, Becks, San Miguel
> Stella, Heineken, Bass as well
>
> I'm still at the pub, still out of me mind
> My best mate Dave, left him behind
> Twelve pints down, no more room
> I'll meet you mate at the Horse and Groom

We filmed a performance of almost every song as soon as we had written it. This led to a massive catalogue of recorded material, the majority being songs we only ever performed once for the original recording. Most Unknown Soldier albums at that time were recorded on a single day in the space of a few hours, the day after one of us asked, "Shall we record a new Soldier album tomorrow?"

It was me, Sadboy and Johnny Butt who were involved with The Best Worst Weekend Ever. We spent a whole Sunday in Johnny Butt's house eating junk and playing video games, getting crippling headaches and feeling like our eyes were bleeding.

Johnny Butt had a SNES and he seemed to only play

Street Fighter IV on it. I took my Mega Drive with a rented copy of Turrican II and I played it all the way through from start to finish in one appalling session that lasted all day. Sadboy spent most of the day laughing at us and taking photos, telling us it was the best worst weekend of his life, after which it went down in history as exactly that.

Meanwhile, back in my day-job, halfway through 1991, when I was an old-hand at being a programmer, a new guy called Ade Wilson joined the IT department and he was given the desk next to me. I suppose they wanted me to show Ade the programming standards and other sensible, work-related stuff, but he mentioned being a guitarist so we never really talked about work much after that. I told him about Unknown Soldier and he asked if I wanted to do some music with him. We used a four-track tape recorder and a better drum machine than the one I used with Unknown Soldier. Ade programmed specific drum patterns for different parts of each song, rather than using the Unknown Soldier method of turning the drum machine on and playing along with a single, looping rhythm. I went back to playing bass with fresh motivation to practice and improve.

For a while, an IT analyst called Diane sat in the desk opposite Ade, and the three of us would play a covert version of the 'Yes/No' game with a 5p stake from each player, the winner taking the whole pot of 15p. The amount wasn't relevant, it was the winning that mattered. In case you don't know how it works, the participants are not allowed to say the words 'yes' or 'no', no matter what, with no excuses or extenuating circumstances. The basic strategy was to stay quiet and get on with your work, which made the game ironically appropriate to play in an office. Of course, we'd try to catch the other players out by asking, "Are we still playing?" or "You're out, aren't you?" but those tricks rarely worked unless something else had happened to distract one or more of the other players. What you really didn't want was a phone call, or a visitor at your desk who wasn't aware of the ongoing yes/no game. There were classic failures, for example when I made it through a long, tedious phone call where I had to answer multiple yes/no questions with replies such as "I can definitely do that", "Certainly, that won't be a problem", and "Not as far as I'm aware" only to put the phone down, punch the air and shout a triumphant "Yes!". Ade and I liked to catch Diane out by accusing her of saying "The 'Y' word" after she came off a phone call or finished talking to someone, because her indignant response was always "No I didn't!".

The first song Ade and I wrote and recorded was called 'Smile'. The lyrics were mostly negative or nihilistic statements, based on the theme of some graffiti I'd seen where someone had written 'Smile, it could be worse' and a reply had been scribbled underneath: 'I did and it was'. Some of the lyrics were: 'My running shoes have the spikes inside', 'I missed my stop on life's bus ride' and 'life looks great when you're out of your tree', but we played it in a bouncy, pop-punk style, taking the piss out of the negativity of the lyrics. The bass part was simple, because I could only play simple bass parts, but it worked really well with Ade's thrashy chords and soloing. We still only had a drum machine, and no singer, but we were inspired enough by the way 'Smile' had turned out to write some more songs. A friend of Ade's, Bruce Juniper, wrote some lyrics for a song called 'Friends (in the basement)'. This was one of the next songs after 'Smile' that we wrote and recorded, in a similarly pop-punk style.

Here are the full 'Smile' lyrics, from our own golden age of writing stupid songs:

> The world could end for all I care
> 'cos life's a party and I've nothing to wear
> My running shoes have the spikes inside
> I missed my stop on life's bus ride

> Smile, gimme gimme a smile…

> A methadone course is prescribed for me
> 'cos life looks great when you're outta your tree
> Next day comes around like a ball and chain
> They're painting smiley faces over my brain

Ade had a room in his house permanently set up with his music and recording equipment, where we played and recorded most of the songs that ended up on our first demo album, but by that time we'd both left the insurance company to go contracting.

Ade left first, and every time we talked on the phone or

got together to play music he would tell me I should go contracting because it was so much better than permie work, and he knew I had enough mainframe programming experience to get some good contracting jobs.

At the time, halfway through the nineties, there were plenty of mainframe IT contracting jobs and there was already a buzz going around about the upcoming century change and all the associated issues with date routines that would need a huge number of analysts and programmers to sort out. I started talking to IT agents who handled contract work, and I had to set up a limited company because of the way the client companies paid contractors via the agencies.

It was a big step, much scarier than just applying for a new job, going out alone into a totally black and white work scenario, where keeping your job was based entirely on your ability to do it. No office politics, no team-building courses, no mind-numbing meetings, just code to write. It made complete sense to me, because it was totally logical. I enjoyed programming, but there was too much bullshit getting in the way of it in a permie office job. When I handed in my notice at the insurance company, and word got out that I was going contracting, one of the managers came up to me and told me there was more to life than money. I smiled at him, said I already knew that, and it was exactly why I was leaving.

My first contract was supposed to be a COBOL programming job with Laurentian Life, another insurance company in Gloucester. The night before I started there, I hadn't been able to sleep and I sat up watching Die Hard on video while my mind went round and round in circles, trying to convince myself I'd done the right thing. On my first day at Laurentian Life, I was asked if I could work on a system I'd never seen before, a letter production application provided by a third-party company which merged data with text to produce the various letters and documents sent out to customers. I had a look at the manuals and some of the programs that sent data to the letter system, and I figured out how it all worked, even though there was hardly any COBOL programming involved.

The Laurentian building was in a business park on the outskirts of Gloucester, three miles from the city centre, but there was a free shuttle bus service running back and forth from the business park to the city bus station between 11 a.m. and 2 p.m. every day. I'd take the bus most days and spend half an hour in Dave Fryer's shop.

I bought most of the consoles and hand-held gaming devices released in the nineties, accumulating a large collection of hardware and games. Johnny Butt and Sadboy started calling me Gary Gadget because I had so much electrical equipment, all the gaming kit and musical gear piled everywhere, plus video recording equipment and even a full drum kit I had set up in my bedroom for a few months.

I had the first model of Gameboy, the one with the monochrome yellow screen, and I played Tetris on it for hours at a time. I'd seen Tetris before, running on a manager's prehistoric PC when I was working in Cardiff with the Civil Service. The Gameboy version was a lot better, perfect on the chunky little handheld console. Now they've gradually reduced Tetris to a pathetic imitation of its earlier incarnations, bogging it down with unnecessary features and irrelevant modes. It could have been fantastic as a phone game, but Electronic Arts got hold of it and cursed it with their inverse Midas touch, the one where everything turns to shit.

I was constantly finding new things to spend my contractor wad on. I bought a NEO-GEO, the original cartridge-format one with an arcade joystick controller that was almost as big as the console itself. The console cost a fortune, but it was the games that were insanely expensive. The niche attraction of the NEO-GEO was the fact that the console cartridges had the same circuit board hardware as the equivalent arcade machines. While this sounded amazing, the sad truth was some of the games weren't that much fun, despite the cost and the arcade heritage. I played a lot of Fatal Fury 2 on it with Sadboy, and we wore out the quote from the intro: "Again, legendary men return", appropriate in many situations involving entering a pub or a fast-food restaurant.

Not long after McDonalds first opened in Hereford, a group of us were in there when Johnny Butt bought a quarter-pounder, took a six-inch nail out of his pocket, slipped it inside between the bun and the meat, and went back to complain about finding a nail in his burger. Sometimes I'd go to the Hereford gym with him on Friday evening, and we'd go to McDonalds after for 'twenty nugs and home'.

I tried eating twenty chicken nuggets and drinking four pints of milk once, and I ended up rolling about on the floor of Johnny Butt's house for an hour with horrible stomach cramps. We did plenty of other things that were just as stupid. I'd get phone calls at home, usually late at night, and when I answered I'd hear Johnny Butt shouting "Badger" before hanging up on me.

He had a black cat called Chairman Miaow, and I'd pick it up and put it on my head with its front legs hanging down like sideburns, then I'd start doing Elvis impersonations while he filmed me. We'd sit in opposite corners on the tiled floor of his kitchen and roll a tennis ball to each other while his cat chased it, sliding about and falling over as it dashed back and forth between us. He filmed it one time, and dubbed the Little Richard song 'Slippin' and Slidin'' over it. He was more than ten years too early for YouTube, and all that priceless footage is long gone now.

Johnny Butt had a tropical fish tank, and he was really into keeping unusual, rare fish. I went to his house one day and he said, "Hey, JT, you've got to see these new fish," and I looked in the tank and there were half a dozen piranha in there, real ones, and I have to say they were ugly looking bastards. Even though we were complete idiots, we never put our fingers in the water to see what might happen.

My three-month contract at Laurentian Life was extended by a month, and then the spike of development activity on their letter system eased off and I had to look for another contract. The mainframe programming job market wasn't showing any sign of slowing down, and I had an offer within a few days of a six-month contract at K3, a software house in Worcester. It was the furthest daily commute I've ever had, a round trip of a hundred miles a day, mostly on the M50 and M5 motorways, but the rate they were paying was a significant increase on my first contract and the work was a constant series of mindless but time-consuming date changes, which was perfect for me.

I wanted to buy an economical car for the daily journey so I had a look at some diesels, such as the Citroen Xantia, but they were all too depressing for me. I went to the big Ford garage in Hereford, still convinced I needed something economical, and I forced myself to consider getting a Mondeo, which had been renamed the Mundano for good reason. While I was trudging along the rows of ex-rental, ex-fleet, loser-mobiles, a chirpy salesman came up to me and started giving me the usual bullshit. By then, I'd had enough of looking at cars, and I told him as much.

"Come and look at this," he said, oblivious to my lack of enthusiasm. He led me to a blue Mondeo parked on its own, outside the main showroom. We walked around the car, and I thought at least it had decent wheels. At the back of the car, the salesman pointed at a small badge underneath the Ford logo: 24V.

"What's that?" I asked.

"Twenty-four valve," the salesman said. He could see I wasn't getting it. "It's a two-point-five litre V6. Six cylinders, twenty-four valves. Ex-demo, only six hundred miles on it."

I told him it didn't sound like the sort of economical commuting car I was looking for, but I was already thinking about the fun I could have in a boring-looking Mondeo with a big V6 engine inside it. The salesman told me I could take it out for a test drive if I wanted to. He knew what he was doing; as soon as I drove onto a straight stretch of road and put my foot down, the sale was as good as done. There was an optional rear spoiler, quite subtle, not too much of a picnic table, and I said yes, stick it on there.

The first day I drove it to K3 in Worcester, a permie bloke who knew more about the different models of Mondeo than I did saw it in the car park and gathered a small crowd around it. I heard them saying it had to be a contractor's car and I admitted that, yes, it was mine. I found the attention awkward, but also amusing, because I'd gone out to buy a slow, boring car, ended up with a fast, boring-looking car, and people were actually impressed by it.

The next thing I blew a pile of contractor cash on was a brand-new Rickenbacker 4003 bass guitar, black body with a white scratch plate. I wanted a Rickenbacker because Lemmy used them, and I liked the way they sounded, more punchy and trebly than the majority of other basses. JJ Burnel mostly played a Fender Precision, and I'd been thinking about getting one of those, but I preferred the look and sound of a Rickenbacker. Buying a new bass gave me fresh motivation to practice the songs I was writing with Ade. We weren't working at the same place, he was at Eagle Star in Cheltenham, but we stayed in touch and we met up on a fairly regular basis to play our songs and write new ones.

I had to quit training at the Kingsholm gym in Gloucester when I was working in Worcester, and I started using a smaller gym in Ross-on-Wye, because Ross was on my route home from Worcester.

For about a year, I was working from nine until half five in Worcester, training in the gym in Ross on the way home, and not getting into the house until about half past eight. This was seriously reducing the amount of gaming time I had in the evenings, but the money more than made up for it, and I was even getting some gaming time in the lunch hours at work due to the unrestricted installation of Windows they were running on the office network.

A few members of the permanent workforce were young graduate kids, and they played Microsoft Hearts on the network in the lunch hour. I got involved with it because there was nothing else to do at lunch time on an industrial estate in Worcester, and I'd always jump at any opportunity to play games on a computer, even a card game that initially looked like something your Granny would play.

Hearts was deceptively brutal, encouraging and rewarding devious, evil tactics. We'd have three or four players on it most lunch times, all sitting at different blocks of desks around the open-plan office. The game involved discarding cards from your hand, trying to end the game without scoring points from picking up any Heart cards or the Queen of Spades. Each turn, going clockwise around the virtual card table, someone would lead with a card, and everyone else would follow. If you had a card of the same suit, you had to play it, otherwise you made a tactical choice about which card you discarded. Whoever played the highest card of the originally dealt suit had to pick up all the discarded cards, scoring one point for any Heart card or thirteen points for the Queen of Spades.

At the end of the game, when a player reached one-hundred points, the player with the lowest accumulated score was the winner. However, if one person managed to score the maximum number of points in a hand, by acquiring every Heart card plus the Queen of Spades, they scored zero and everyone else had the maximum number of points added to their overall score. If you noticed someone trying to do the 'high score' trick, it was always a whole load of fun to deliberately lose a turn to wreck their plans, particularly if you gambled and waited until late in the hand to unleash the surprise upset. The graduate kids really didn't like losing, and they would swear and smack their mouse against the desk, and then have to make up a story about writing bad code or accidentally deleting something to explain the outburst, while the other Hearts players leaned around their monitors and laughed at them.

One of the older K3 permies had internet access on his work PC, which was a big deal in 1995, and he downloaded Hexen and put it on a network drive where I could find it and install it. I didn't play it much because I was a true professional with a laudable work ethic (didn't want to get sacked), but it was impressive that we had access to real games on our work computers.

The PlayStation felt like a big gamble, a lot of money to spend on a console from a company making a bid to break into an industry already dominated by several established huge names such as Sega and Nintendo. I bought one as soon as it came out in September 1995.

The following week, I took it to Ade Wilson's house on my way home after work, with the three games I'd bought with it: Ridge Racer, Tekken and Wipeout. Ade had a little two-storey, two-bedroom house in Abbeydale, one of the big, sprawling estate areas in Gloucester, so it was a bit of a detour off my normal route home. His neighbours on one side ran a bouncy castle rental company, so there was always some sort of chaos going on in their garden.

Ade and I played each of the three PlayStation games, amazed at the speed of the 3D graphics in Ridge Racer and Wipeout. Ade had been thinking about getting a PlayStation, but he wanted to see mine before making a decision. My attitude was: it's a new gaming gadget, therefore I will buy it.

Ade was into Oasis, and he had their 'What's The Story' album playing while we were on the PlayStation. I never really liked Oasis; I was still mostly listening to punk bands and Motorhead, always will be, and I thought Oasis were a bit safe and commercial, and a bit whiny. I also wasn't into Blur, so I suppose I was an equal opportunities nineties music disliker.

I never felt massively let down by a PlayStation game, and some of them were truly incredible. Blood Omen: Legacy of Kain came out in 1996. I was hooked on the premise before

I even saw the game. You played a tragic anti-hero who starts the game getting brutally killed in a cut-scene, then brought back to life as a vampire. You wander around being generally bloodthirsty and vicious, never allowed to forget that you're not exactly the good guy. Whacking things with a big sword, combined with sucking blood out of injured enemies, was an endless source of grisly entertainment. While it wasn't a full-on RPG, there were a couple of basic stats to increase and a strong sense of progression as you gradually became more powerful.

Crusader: No Remorse was a nice PC-gaming surprise in 1995, with the sequel, which felt like a standalone expansion pack, Crusader: No Regret, cashing in on the first game's success a year later. The game was an isometric shooter, a niche genre that hasn't been exploited anywhere near as much as it should have been. The story was the basic formula of 'bad-guy gets shafted by his evil masters and switches sides to help the resistance' and the player character wore a red robot-armour suit that 'looked a bit like' (rather than 'was a blatant copy of') Boba Fett, particularly the helmet, which is virtually identical.

In the first Crusader game, and not so much the second, there were lots of environmental elements that could be used to complete objectives in different ways. Okay, I say 'in different ways' but this was generally limited to shooting things, blowing things up, using remote-controlled spider mines to blow things up, and hacking ED-209 lookalike robots and using them to shoot things or blow them up. But it was all excellent fun, despite the way I'm describing it. Some of the guns were brutally hilarious. There was a freeze gun, to freeze people so they could subsequently be shattered. The flame gun burned those suckers up. A zappy people-frying gun, I think this was called the microwave projector, gave predictably grim results. And there was some kind of toxic glop gun, which melted people into goo, with lots of flailing and screaming involved. There was also a UV gun that flayed enemies down to their skeletons. Because we're relying on my memory for most of this, I can't say for sure which of those guns only showed up in the second game, but does it matter? No, not really.

Tomb Raider came out in 1996 but I didn't get it on the PlayStation because it came out on PC at the same time, and my PC was capable of running it. I knew this in advance, because they put out a pre-release demo of it for the PC. Back in the nineties, there were a lot of pre-release demos for big games, some doing the shareware thing like Doom, others just putting out a free demo that was separate from the full game.

The demo for Carmageddon was included on a PC magazine coverdisc in 1997 (I think it was PC Zone but I'm not absolutely sure), and I played that demo more than I played some full games. Of course, when the full version of Carmageddon was released it had been neutered by the censors, and the release was an infamous shambles, the game only being salvaged back to something approaching its former glory by the notorious Splat Pack patch that reinstated red blood among other things.

Tomb Raider was a hard game. People seem to forget that now, after all the sequels and the tie-in movies, the various hyped-up controversies about triangular boobs and the representation of women in video games. When Tomb Raider came out, we all knew what it was: an Indiana Jones rip-off aimed squarely at the target demographic. But, rather than fuss and moan about all that, we got on with it and tried to reach the part with the T-Rex as quickly as possible. The thing I most remember about Tomb Raider is getting stuck on puzzles, over and over again, and spending ages backtracking through a cleared-out level looking for something I must have missed. It was a fun game but it was a frustrating game, not just the pioneer of the third-person 3D puzzle-em-up, but the pioneer of the casual gamer's absolute reliance on a step-by-step walkthrough. A puzzle involving collecting cogwheels particularly sticks in my mind, that and deliberately jumping into a pit full of spikes, over and over again, when I got utterly fed up with looking for the last one.

Like Nintendo and its exclusive games, Sony had some games that only came out on the PlayStation. The best example I can think of is Gran Turismo. The first one was my favourite, I never liked the changes they introduced with the sequels. By the time Johnny Butt bought a PlayStation and Gran Turismo, I was much further into the game and I'd unlocked loads of special cars that you could only get from completing specific races.

Gran Turismo had a unique feature using the PlayStation's memory card: a player could save their garage of cars onto a memory card, then transfer one or more cars to another player's garage of cars. I don't remember the exact details of how this worked, but the original memory card kept the car, and the destination memory card got a duplicate car for the other player.

I gave Johnny Butt a race-spec Mitsubishi FTO which was a sort of cheat car because you could use it in some races where its vehicle type 'FF' (forward engine, front-wheel drive) wouldn't normally be eligible to compete. It was a crazy car, very fast, and almost impossible to spin out or crash unless you were a complete idiot. Like most of the race-spec cars in the game, you could only get the FTO by completing a really hard series of races.

There was a race-spec Porsche that you got if you won an endurance race that lasted something like three real-time hours. It was totally draining, I'd start drifting off the track and making stupid mistakes due to staring at the screen for ages and developing a kind of mutant-claw hand affliction from holding the controller for too long in one session. The only way I could deal with it was by pausing the game and taking a break for a few minutes, making a cup of coffee and mentally preparing myself before un-pausing the game. There was no option to shorten the endurance races, you just had to do it. Or not. Yoda would have been a huge fan of Gran Turismo.

My two favourite cars, apart from the race-spec FTO, were the Nissan Skyline and the Dodge Viper. There was a race challenge for unmodified rear-wheel drive cars, which meant you had to use the car in its default state: all standard parts, and standard tyres. From a straight-line speed perspective, the Viper was the car to go for. From a 'spinning out of control on every corner' perspective, you wouldn't lose money betting on the Viper to do that. What I had to do was practice, practice, practice. Just like in real life, assuming you've got an infinite supply of Dodge Vipers and some extensive medical insurance.

I wanted to win the race, and I knew the Viper could do it. There was no question about the car being fast enough, it was the driver that failed every time on one of the particularly treacherous turns. But I didn't quit. I started the race and I spun out and I restarted and got further through the race and I spun out and I restarted, over and over.

It was grinding, but with no in-game progress. The progress was all on me. I got better at driving the unmodified Dodge Viper, better at timing the braking, better at accelerating out of bends. I controlled the fish-tailing and the skidding, and I stopped doing all the spin-outs. I got much better at driving the Dodge Viper around that track. It took many hours, over several days. I hadn't put that much effort and dedication into a real-life activity outside the gym. The other cars in the race were all driven by competent AI, but they weren't practising and improving, they were stuck at their pre-programmed ability levels.

Instead of spinning out for last place, I drove a careful race and finished in the bottom five. A few hours later I drove a quicker race, trimming tenths of seconds off each corner, braking later and later, and I finished in the top five. Finally, in one never-to-be-repeated race where every corner was executed perfectly, every touch of the virtual brake pedal was as late as it could possibly be, and if I'd gone any faster at any point I would have spun off the track, I scraped a first-place finish, dripping with sweat and shaking like a shitting dog. I can't remember what the prize was for winning the race, probably a decent car, but I was way more interested in winning the race than getting the prize.

I put a set of grippy tyres and some upgraded brakes on the Viper and I went out and won a whole bunch of rear-wheel drive races after that. I had learned how to drive the car. It had been tough and it had taken a long time, but I had done it. That's why Gran Turismo had the subtitle The Real Driving Simulator; it wasn't an arcade car game, it was a driving sim.

The most recent driving sim I've played is American Truck Simulator, and I hardly ever spin out on a tight corner driving a Peterbilt eighteen-wheeler. Hardly ever.

In 1986, Diablo changed everything. If you look at the impact Doom had on video game evolution, it was huge, and there were countless first-person shooter games released in Doom's wake that were labelled as Doom clones. The same thing happened with Diablo, and the labelling of a game as a Diablo clone has lasted more than twenty years, with the term still being widely used these days, and I'd bet there are people using the term today who never even played the original Diablo. It's like tagging 'gate' on the end of something to indicate a scandal or an online muppet-fest, without knowing anything about the Nixon-era Watergate scandal.

Before Diablo, there had been no similar action role-playing games. I'd played Dungeon Master on the Atari ST, Elder Scrolls: Arena on the PC, various other RPGs that all followed the same general gameplay blueprint. Diablo broke the rules. It made the action, meaning the wholesale slaughter of millions of enemies, the focus of the gameplay, with every other feature of the game supporting this or playing much less of a significant part than in a traditional CRPG.

There were hardly any NPCs, the quests were all 'go to the next place and kill everything' or subtle variations on that recurring theme. The main quest involved going somewhere to kill something big and nasty. You couldn't walk more than a yard in any direction without getting into a fight. You couldn't solve any problems with speech or charisma or diplomacy, you had to step up and smack evil in the face with a big axe, or a sword, a volley of arrows, or a fireball. Peace through superior firepower. Want to be a healer? Go play another game.

Diablo taught us to maximise our damage per second, to kite, and to obsessively collect loot. Entire universes were born from the game's 'Stay awhile and listen' quote. In the field of genre-defining classics, Diablo set the standard and we're still waiting for a more influential game to come along.

Near the end of the thirteen months I was working at K3, the film Scream had its cinema release. A few of the graduate kids told me they were going to watch it on the opening weekend, and I'd already booked my ticket to see it on Saturday night. The following Monday, all of us who had seen it were talking about the film, and agreeing that Beth, one of the permie analysts, was a dead ringer for Sidney Prescott, the character played by Neve Campbell. The face and hair similarities were uncanny, and she even smiled like Neve. The funniest thing I saw Beth do was shout "Fuck!" really loudly when someone crept up behind her while she was working at her desk, blew up a big paper bag and popped it.

My own K3 contracting bubble burst when the company they were doing all the date changes for went out of business. Without that client, the K3 workload dropped massively and they gave all the contractors their agreed notice periods. Not everyone's was the same, because different agencies had different agreements, and mine was an extravagant four-week notice period, which meant I was going to get paid for four weeks while they had no work to give me. I went in every day, picking up scraps of work from whoever needed help, mostly Beth because of my Neve Campbell obsession, filling the remaining hours by quietly playing Hearts against the computer.

While I was waiting for the four-week notice period to run out, I phoned Laurentian Life to see if they had any contracting work. "We were going to give you a call," they said. "When can you start?"

Chapter 9

The end of the century
'Stay awhile, and listen.'

By the mid-nineties, video game arcades were dead and buried, gone forever, either closed down or mutated into money-grabbing fruit machine dens. Everyone was playing video games at home, on consoles and PCs, and there were loads of great games being released, so fast that there was no way to keep up and play every good game on every platform, even if you were a lottery winner or a mainframe IT contractor surfing the tsunami of millennium bug fixes.

I'll take a moment here to set a few things straight about the millennium bug, good old Y2K, because I see a lot of nonsense being spouted online these days by know-it-all muppets who weren't even out of their Pampers pull-ups in the late nineties. They post sweeping generalisations on social media, telling the world that Y2K was a joke, that the millennium bug didn't exist, that people back in the nineties were silly old boomers, that we fell for the century date bug scaremongering because we were gullible fools. Well, you weren't there, chum, and you're just copy-pasting a load of fake-hindsight drivel from some other pillock's misinformed Facebook posts. Here you go, the truth about the millennium bug, from someone who was there, and who fixed his fair share of turn-of-the-century date problems…

Between the sixties and the eighties, storage on mainframe computer systems wasn't cheap. Most computer systems used by businesses recorded dates, lots and lots of dates. Customer date of birth, the date an insurance policy started, the date a claim was made, the date any transaction occurred on a policy, or a bank account, or pretty much anything. It made sense to store the dates in a six-character format such as YYMMDD, which was the optimum format for calculations. Hardly anyone included the century, because it was unnecessary. It was always 19. It was never going to change. Ever. Well, not for several decades, and the IT guys back then were far more concerned about saving storage space than worrying about what might happen in the far distant future of the twenty-first century, when they would probably be retired anyway, and it would be someone else's problem to sort out.

At some point during the nineties, people working in banks and insurance companies and government departments started asking this question: "What will our date calculations do when the year changes from ninety-nine to double-zero?". The date fields held the year, not the century, which was fine as long as all the dates on the system were in the twentieth century, with the same implied century value. For example, you might have had a customer-details screen where you typed in a date of birth, and the screen logic had a bit of basic validation to check whether the customer was over eighteen by subtracting the date of birth from the current date. If the current date was the twelfth of March 1996, held on the computer as 960312, and you typed in a birth-date of the twentieth of July 1958, the computer validation would subtract 580720 from 960312 and the birth-date would be passed as valid.

On the same system, after the century clocked over from 19 to 20, the year of the current date would change from 99 to 00. I'd clocked Space Invaders past 9990 enough times to see how that was going to work. From the first of January 2000, the existing validation that checked a date of birth would no longer work in a comparison against a birth-date from the previous century. Get your calculator out and subtract 580720 from 960312. You get 379592. The difference in years is 37. Now, see what happens when you try to subtract 580720 from 000101, which is how the first of January 2000 would be held in a six-digit date field in YYMMDD format. Yeah. Not so good. You get a weird negative value.

Without a fix, without the basic inclusion of a century value to both dates, nobody's twentieth century date of birth would pass the validation that had worked fine up to the last day of 1999. Now, take that little problem and multiply it by every date comparison and calculation on every company and government's computer systems in the whole world. And that was Y2K, that was the millennium bug, explained quite well if I say so myself. You're welcome.

Laurentian Life wanted me back because they were being rebranded as Lincoln Insurance. It might have been a takeover, or a merger, I honestly can't remember, but the company name was changing and they needed someone to find and replace every logo and every instance of the company name scattered throughout their various computer systems and applications. It was like a dry-run for fixing the millennium bug, but with a cartoon tree (the old Laurentian logo) and a silhouette profile picture of Lincoln (Abraham, although it looked more like Jimmy Hill or Bruce Forsyth) instead of years and centuries.

The Lincoln logo was the source of much amusement due to the resemblance to Jimmy Hill. It was just the chin, but that was enough. It would have been fine in America, because they wouldn't have known who Jimmy Hill was, but in Gloucester we knew, and we laughed.

The first game I played online, albeit only on a direct modem-to-modem connection over the phone line, was Duke Nukem 3D. One of the other contractors at Laurentian was a bloke called Tom, and he was into the same sort of video games as me. We both had Duke Nukem 3D and we'd both completed the single-player campaign. I'd started creating levels using the editor that came with the game, and I wanted to play online to try some of my homemade levels out against a human opponent.

Duke Nukem 3D had daft enemies, puerile 'adult' content, cool one-liners lifted straight out of some of my favourite films, and laser tripwire mines that were hilarious in one-on-one deathmatch games. It was a great game.

Another landmark first-person shooter came out in 1996, and that was Quake. It was far more serious than Duke Nukem 3D, darker in both style and theme, with rusting, ancient-looking environments and gruesome enemies. It was id Software's follow-up to Doom, and for that reason alone it could do no wrong as far as the majority of reviewers and FPS fans were concerned. The review in PC Zone magazine gave it a massive score and a summary tagline of 'Fucking brilliant'. I liked PC Zone, it was informative and rebellious, and it had Charlie Brooker, who was reliably outspoken and opinionated. I had a few letters printed in PC Zone, and I won a review-writing competition in 2000 with a review of Soldier of Fortune, another first-person shooter, which was controversial at the time due to the realistic dismemberments and extreme levels of violence. The prize for that competition was a SIM motor scooter, complete with a full year's insurance. I rode it around for a couple of weeks before I got bored of it and sold it to a motorcycle dealer in Hereford.

My contract at Laurentian was extended to six months from the original three. They kept finding more and more potential date issues, and the contractors were working flat-out rewriting code and building new versions of data files to accommodate the longer date fields with the century values included.

One of my fellow contractors there was a bossy know-it-all called Anne. She loved telling the rest of us the best way to do everything, in the most patronising way possible. I found out her car registration, and I'd occasionally tell the receptionist on the front desk that someone had left their headlights on, and I'd give them Anne's car registration as a bit of a prank. Pathetic and juvenile, granted, but still rewardingly amusing. They'd announce it on the office tannoy system and she'd go out to turn her lights off, then she'd come back in ten minutes later, looking rather confused. One time when I did it, she looked confused before she even went outside. "I'm not in my car today, I'm using my husband's," she said, and then she went outside to check anyway. Not the brightest pixel on the screen, our Anne.

At the end of the six-month contract, I went to the pub for a farewell drink with a group of permies and some of the contractors. While we were there, Chris, the manager I was working for, came up to me and asked if he could have a word. "We'd like you to stay on, maybe for another six months," he said. They were looking at the amount they were spending on software licences, and the third-party letter system I'd previously worked on was costing them a quarter of a million every year. Chris asked me if I thought I could write a replacement system, and I said I could. I'd already been reverse-engineering the existing system as a kind of side-hobby in my lunch hours, creating stand-alone programs that replicated parts of the letter production process because it was easier to test letter changes that way than by trying to run the whole process.

When I turned up the following Monday, quite a few

people were surprised to see me because they thought I'd left, and they told me they wouldn't be going to my next leaving do because I'd probably just come back again straight after it.

What do you think of when someone says 1997? If you're a gamer, more specifically a PC gamer, and you like post-apocalypse themed role-playing games with turn-based combat, you're going to be jumping up and down, waving your claw-like mouse-clutching hand, and you're going to be shouting one word, over and over: Fallout.

It really was as original and influential as they all say it was, tough too, and with its own ultra-dark humour and a lot of moments where you sat there looking at the screen, thinking this is some grim shit going on here. A year later, the sequel proved how restrained the first game had been, with more mutants, more opportunities to screw everyone over, and even the chance to be a fluffer on a porn movie set. I got hooked on Fallout and Fallout 2, completed them both, and spent far too many hours out there in the wasteland looking for mutants to slaughter and innocents to rob. Although nobody in the Fallout wasteland was ever truly innocent.

1997 saw the release of another game that not only launched its own massively successful franchise, but also started an entire genre of open-world shenanigans that didn't involve swords, sorcery, and glitchy dragons. Games in the genre have frequently taken place in a contemporary setting, although not exclusively, and cars have been a very prominent feature.

Obviously, I'm talking about Grand Theft Auto. Not so

obviously, I'm talking about the original GTA that came out in 1997, not GTA 3 which was the first game in the series to be in the third-person, three-dimensional view we all now associate with the genre. Grand Theft Auto was a top-down game, and it was great fun.

During one of our planned music days, when we should have been writing and rehearsing Dum songs, Ade brought his PC to my house and we connected it to my PC to try out some local multiplayer Grand Theft Auto. Any possibility of practising our songs went right out the window as we spent the whole time chasing each other around the top-down view of the city, running each other over with buses and blowing vehicles up with rocket launchers. It was ridiculously fun, totally stupid and over the top, just the way a video game should be.

Writing a version of the existing letter system for Lincoln Insurance was the most fun I've had in work, not counting the time I hid a manager's desk and chair during a big refurbishment, but that was back at the first Gloucester insurance company, when I was young and impetuous. He got really upset when he couldn't find his desk, and some people did a reasonable job of pretending to think it wasn't funny.

The first project manager in charge of my letter system rewrite at Lincoln bailed out when I told him how I planned to fit an estimated twelve months' work into the six months they gave me to do it. I said we'd put the core programs live and deploy the programs for each letter as and when they were ready, with minimal testing. In the mornings, we'd get a few people to check the printed letters. If any looked wrong, I'd make the program corrections and re-run programs that needed running before reprinting the letters. I knew we'd have time to get it all done in the mornings before the post was collected, and we didn't have time to fully test everything in advance. Of course, the whole 'not testing' plan scared the hell out of the bloke, and he left the project to go and do something less likely to permanently tarnish his managerial reputation.

Chris, the manager I'd previously worked for, took over the project. He asked me what I needed, and I said I just needed to get stuff done, with no interference. I said if I messed it up, they could always refuse to pay me. I also told him I could give all the programs that dealt with each individual letter to the junior programmers to write. It would be like a factory production line, all coding and no bullshit. I ended up with five or six eager, wary young programmers and I told them not to worry about all the stuff they'd heard about putting programs live without them being tested.

During my continually extended contract at Lincoln, which didn't finish until close to the end of November 1999, Ade and I wrote and recorded enough songs to be able to put a selection of the ones we liked the most on a demo CD. One of Ade's friends, a bloke called Digger, recorded all the vocals for us; he was a really good singer, from more of a choir background than punk rock, but he was a much better singer than either of us so the vocals were actually in tune, and overall he did a great job on all the songs.

Ade copied a pile of CDs on his PC and I printed the labels and the CD case inlays, and we gave copies to anyone who showed the slightest interest in the band. By that time, the band was called Dum. Ade chose the name, based on the song 'Dumb' from Nirvana's 1993 album, In Utero, with the 'b' removed for artistic reasons, explained by Ade as "It makes the name look even more dumb."

The Stinky Banana Demo is a quirky collection of early incarnations of Dum songs. Some were slow versions of the songs they would eventually become, and others never evolved beyond that point. The drum machine kept perfect time and never tried to convince me that Marillion wasn't a crap band, but there was something about having the same artificial, electronic drumming on each track that sterilised the demo CD and made it feel like a collection of karaoke covers of songs that might have been good with a real drummer. The irony of that became clear when a real drummer decided to join the band after listening to the Stinky Banana Demo, but that was far, far away in the distant future of the next century.

The last big thing I bought while I was contracting was a Chevrolet Camaro Z28, a black one, brand new from a Vauxhall GM garage in Bristol in the summer of 1998. There was a period of a few years in the late nineties when a number of Vauxhall GM garages in Britain sold Camaros and Corvettes. They weren't right-hand drive UK models like the Mustangs you can get nowadays, they were left-hand drive with just a few modifications to the exhaust to meet whatever tree-hugging regulations the EU was imposing at the time.

The Corvette was out of my price range, or I would have bought one of those, but the Camaro was something I could afford. I'd always liked the idea of owning an American muscle car, specifically a Pontiac Trans-Am, but I'd been using a Camaro quite a lot in Gran Turismo and I loved the look of the 1998 model when I went down to Bristol to see it in the GM garage showroom.

The day I collected my new Camaro, I drove down to Bristol with Smiley. I followed the advice given by Chuck Berry in the song 'No Money Down' by trading in my Ford, which in my case was the 24V Mondeo. The Camaro was nuts, a 5.7 litre V8 engine attached to a big, heavy, cruise-missile chassis, capable of doing nought to sixty about as quickly as a Porsche, but with the same steering and suspension technology as on the cars Chuck Berry was singing about in the fifties.

The fastest car I'd previously owned was a Toyota Supra. I wrote that car off in 1990 by aquaplaning it into several piles of cast-iron manhole covers and half a ton of pipes stacked on the side of the road while I was driving home from Johnny Butt's house at half one in the morning in a rainstorm. I promised myself I'd stick to the speed limit in the Camaro, if it was raining heavily.

Not many people knew what kind of car it was, and I'd get blokes coming up to me at petrol stations and in car parks, asking about it. Most of the time they thought the left-hand drive was a big turn-off, but I got used to it and never found it to be much of a problem.

The new Camaro caused a bit of a stir at Lincoln Insurance, more evidence the contractors were a bunch of overpaid boy racers. Michelle, one of the junior programmers, was really into American cars; she and her boyfriend both drove imports. "You know the Camaro is a girl's car, don't you?" she said to me. I gave her the keys and asked her if she wanted to take it for a drive around the bypass. When she came back, she said it was okay but it was still a girl's car.

PC gaming was exploding in 1998. Half-Life came out and we had to drastically revise our expectations of first-person shooters. Doom was ancient history, a clunky five-year-old relic from prehistoric times. The advances in gaming development since 1993 were phenomenal; we could walk underneath platforms in three dimensions in 1998, and in Doom we hadn't been able to do that. Half-Life introduced the crowbar as an iconic video game melee weapon, and it also introduced Gordon Freeman, a zero-to-hero protagonist, the extra name I would regularly add to sign-in lists at corporate events after I made my reluctant return to permie office life in the next century. Half-Life was great, almost as good as most people say it was; I always thought the final section was disappointing compared to the rest of the game, and the unsatisfactory final boss-fight against a giant alien potato felt like a proper let-down at the time.

I got into Buffy the Vampire Slayer late, by about a year,

had to play catch-up on the first series, and then watched every episode from season two onwards on the day it was aired, or the following day if I was going out that evening and had to video it. I had a Nokia mobile phone, the first one with the Snake game on it, and the phone had a basic composer built into it where you could write your own ringtone music. I found the music notation for the Buffy theme online and I spent ages in the composer setting it up as the ringtone on my phone. Of course, the phone companies realised they could make money from selling ringtones, and nobody included a composer application with a phone ever again. They told us 'Home taping is killing music' back in the eighties, but I support the counter argument that institutionalised greed kills fun. Every time.

Talking of fun, also getting back to what I'm supposed to be writing about, PC gamers were overloaded with excellent games in 1998. Half-Life led a stellar cast of landmark titles such as Baldur's Gate, Starcraft, and Thief: The Dark Project. Imagine a single year with that many hugely influential games being released, it sounds crazy now.

Half-Life redefined the first-person shooter, Baldur's Gate took the Dungeons and Dragons rulebook and made a truly legendary computer role-playing game out of it, Starcraft set a whole new standard for real-time strategy games, and Thief gave us a chance to sneak about in the dark, eavesdropping on guards and shooting noisemaker arrows, in the game that did more than any other to define the massively popular stealth sub-genre.

Thief was a lot of fun, until the later parts of the game where it changed into a frustrating slog fighting zombies, with none of the stealth and robbery that made the first half so entertaining. I don't know whether they'd always planned to have it devolve into a tedious zombie-fest (years before zombies were a tired gaming trope) or if they had to pad the game out with undead brawling because it was too short. Whatever the reason, the zombie nonsense didn't really suit the theme or the stealth gameplay.

These days, we're all familiar with stealth games but, when Thief came out, all the first-person games up to then had focussed on fighting enemy characters. Thief broke that mould, giving us a game world, objectives, and skills that made us avoid enemies, hide from them, and distract them. If you went in, guns blazing, which you couldn't do anyway because you didn't have any guns, you'd fail dismally. Sneaking about was a whole lot of fun.

The bow in Thief had a few different types of ammunition, for example the water arrows could be shot at burning torches to extinguish them. The real enemy in Thief was light, or more specifically, being in or near any areas of light. One tactic that never stopped being fun was to sneak from one guard to another, luring each one into a dark area, clubbing them unconscious and hiding the body. The same basic gameplay has been repeated in many games since then, with all sorts of tweaks and enhancements but still the core stealth-thrills of hiding from armed guards, silently eliminating them, and stashing their bodies out of sight.

First-person and third-person viewpoint games, even entire franchises, that immediately come to mind for their stealth gameplay include Deus Ex, Splinter Cell, Hitman, Tenchu, Assassin's Creed, Skyrim, Dishonored, and Kingdom Come Deliverance. Thief wasn't the only game in the late nineties with stealth elements, and 1998 seems to stand out as the year when the genre really took off. Since then, I've lost count of the number of times I've been sneaking about in the dark, in a game, and someone has walked up behind me, or just spoken to me, in the real world, and I've screamed like an electrocuted baby.

Unreal appeared in a co-starring role, not exactly blowing anyone's mind, although it was a decent first-person shooter, but a year later they'd add the word 'Tournament' to the sequel's name and that would be a whole different story.

If I had to pick a favourite PC game from 1998, and I already told you I change my mind about favourites as soon as I choose one, I'd say it was Commandos: Behind Enemy Lines. It was a bloody hard game, a real test of patience, planning, timing, and a whole lot of covert corpse disposal. It took me ages to figure out how to not totally screw up the first mission, but that was all part of the game's appeal. Beating each mission felt like a real accomplishment, a triumph of skill, tactics and, of course, stashing a huge pile of bodies. Graphically, it looked a bit like Fallout, but it was a totally different type of game. The real-time tactical genre it pioneered has never been one of the most massively popular or successful, but it produced some classic games, such as

Desperados: Wanted Dead or Alive that came out in 2001.

One of the magazine reviews, most likely PC Zone's, described Commandos as the perfect game for angry loners. I remember reading that review after I'd already been playing the game for a while, and loving it, and I had to agree with them.

The internal computer network at Lincoln Insurance was light years ahead of the non-existent network ten years earlier when I was in the Civil Service, but there was still only rudimentary IT Security and no external internet access. We had email, but we could only use it between internal email addresses on the company network. I took a disk with Simpsons screensavers on it into work and installed it on my PC. The best one on there was Itchy and Scratchy. People would see it running on my computer and ask if they could have it. It ended up on dozens of PCs there, and I started noticing it running on machines in different departments when I was wandering around the building. Life finds a way, we'd been told by Jeff Goldblum in 1993, but unapproved software installations of illegally copied screensavers were even more adept at finding a way.

Microsoft Arcade had come out in 1993, and it was a great little collection of classic arcade games, including my all-time favourite: Asteroids. I gave a copy of Microsoft Arcade to Phil, one of the junior programmers at Lincoln, and he got told off for playing on it in work. You had to at least try to be subtle, or have a desk where the monitor faced a wall, where nobody could walk up behind you and catch you off guard.

Attaching wing mirrors to the monitor is a bit excessive; I've seen it done, but never quite gone to those extreme lengths myself.

Phil was a decent kid, he started hanging around in the smoking room because he fancied one of the girls who smoked in there. I thought that sounded like true love, because the smoking room was a grim place to go for a non-smoker. They got together, and later got married while I was still working at Lincoln. I went to the wedding, at a hotel near Castle Combe, and it was a pretty good day although I forgot to bring a change of clothes for the evening do, and I ended up taking a shower in another wedding guest's hotel room and spending most of the evening with her. Funny how things turn out sometimes.

Chapter 10
Never play in hardcore mode
'Get back to work, you slacker!'

From late November 1999 to early September 2000 I was out of work. Towards the end of 1999, most companies stopped making changes to their computer systems in preparation for the century switch. At Lincoln Insurance all the date fixes had been applied and tested, and I'd finished documenting the replacement letter system. There was nothing left to do, so they didn't extend my contract, or anyone else's, and we all drifted away with the intention of getting back into a big post-Y2K clean-up operation in the new century.

It didn't happen. There might have been a few places where a bug or two made it through, but the widespread combination of financial paranoia and extreme risk-mitigation code fixes sorted out the vast majority of date issues in advance. I phoned Lincoln in January 2000 and they told me, sorry, but we're not taking any contractors on at the moment. My long-term contract there had been great while it lasted, but it meant I hadn't worked anywhere else since I left K3 more than three years earlier. I couldn't go back to K3 because the company no longer existed after being assimilated by IBM. I kept trying to find another mainframe programming contract but there was nothing local, and hardly anything even way beyond what I considered to be a realistic commuting distance.

For the first few months of 2000, I wasn't particularly bothered. I'd saved plenty of money, even after buying the Camaro and enough hi-tech gadgets to fill a dozen Bat Caves, and I was certain something good would turn up. I had plenty of things to fill my time, enough that I didn't think I could have also fitted a full-time job in there.

Dum found a drummer, or maybe Joel found us, I can't remember exactly how it happened; he was either a friend-of-a-friend of Ade's, or a friend-of-a-friend of Ade's wife. He'd been given a copy of the Stinky Banana demo and he liked it enough to want to join the band. Ade found a rehearsal studio in Cheltenham and the three of us went there to see how it worked out playing some of our songs with a real drummer. It was amazing, a genuinely fantastic experience.

All the Stinky Banana karaoke tracks that sounded okay with a drum machine became real songs, instantly, with a jaw-dropping urgency and power I'd never suspected we were capable of producing. It was fun playing with a real drummer, proper laugh-out-loud fun, and it sounded like a real band, not a couple of blokes recording on a four-track with a drum machine. In my mind I was back on the start line of a forty-bike motocross race, with the ten-second board up and every engine screaming as the clutches dropped.

I don't remember ever having a conversation with Ade

after that session in the rehearsal studio, about whether or not we wanted Joel to join the band. He turned up and we played together, and that was it, he was in. Dum sounded too good with Joel drumming for there to be any question about whether we wanted him in, and Joel liked the daft songs with silly lyrics because he'd already been in too many serious bands.

I stuck to a routine on weekdays, driving to the gym in Ross every afternoon to train with Cliff Hall, a local legend of weight training, one of the most genuine, no-nonsense blokes I've ever met. Cliff was big, extremely strong, a real larger-than-life character and a great training partner. A lot of the real-life stories he told me formed the basis for a major character in my seventh novel, Old Scars, the sequel to Cold Inside.

The rest of the time, I played a lot of video games. I also started writing a fantasy novel, which I finished but probably won't ever try to publish because it's not very good. Writing it helped pass the time. Sometimes that's all a writing project is good for, and sometimes that's enough.

The first year of the twenty-first century produced a lot of memorable games, as if game companies had been deliberately saving their latest, greatest innovations for the new century.

And the sequels. Don't forget the sequels. On the PC we had Diablo 2, Deus Ex, Baldur's Gate 2, Escape from Monkey Island, Soldier of Fortune, Icewind Dale, Project IGI, John Romero's anticlimactic letdown: Daikatana, The

Sims, Command and Conquer: Red Alert, and Hitman: Codename 47. Looking at that list, I'm glad I didn't have a job for most of 2000 because I would have had to miss out on more than half the decent games released that year.

If I have to choose one of them as the highlight game of 2000, I'm going to go with Deus Ex. The demo was brilliant; I played it over and over, trying out everything possible and a whole load of things that might not have been possible but the game let you try them anyway. There was a difficulty mode beyond easy, normal and hard called 'Realistic' which pretty much meant you died if you got shot once, but so did everyone else, and this really appealed to me. Not because I'm a raging masochist but because it was so unflinchingly fair, and it was also a real test of your gaming skills. Deus Ex deserved all the critical praise and awards it received.

After playing the Deus Ex demo a million times, I couldn't wait to get hold of the full game, and I mean I literally could not wait. The game was due out on a Saturday, in the middle of June. I drove into Hereford on the Friday afternoon before release day, went into one of the independent game shops and asked them if they were going to be selling Deus Ex the next day. They said they were. I asked if they'd have copies for sale first thing in the morning. They said they would, because the stock had already been delivered. I asked if I could buy one right then, on Friday afternoon, because I wouldn't be able to come into town the next day. They said no. I asked again, more begging than asking, promising I wouldn't tell anyone, promising I wouldn't install the game until Saturday morning. Eventually, probably just to get the hopeless, whining loser out of the shop, they sold me Deus Ex the day before its official release date. I took it home, installed it and started playing it. Excellent game, definitely one of my top ten favourites of all time.

Stealth and sniping in Deus Ex weren't essential, but they were insanely fun. There was a quest involving rescuing cats, or maybe it was avenging dead cats, but you didn't find out it was cats until you completed the mission, the quest-giver calling them by name and never mentioning they were cats and not people. That weird quest sticks in my mind more than any of the nanotech upgrades or character skills.

Talking of character skills, Baldur's Gate 2 was an excellent sequel, a fabulous RPG with some ridiculously tough enemies and emotionally tough story twists involving members of the protagonist's party. Standout memory, apart from the big bald bloke with the pet mouse - Go for the eyes, Boo, go for the eyes! - is finding a belt with a flat 19 Strength attribute (19 is the maximum attribute level in BG2) in a shop, realising it was always going to be there, starting a new game and lowering the main character's strength as far as it would go during character creation to redistribute the points in other attributes, struggling and save-spamming all the way to the shop, buying the belt and ending up with an overpowered super-character. Not that this actually made the game any easier, but it was fun to do after figuring it out myself.

I liked Project IGI despite all its faults, most memorably the infinitely respawning enemies. It was predominantly a sniper game, and the sniping was really well done and hugely entertaining.

The original Hitman game was an inconsistent mixed bag of glorious, satisfying headshots and glitchy, ill-conceived levels that looked like Doom and Tomb Raider started a fight in a jungle after doing too much bad acid. People think I look like Agent 47, or he looks like me, and I'm thinking I could have used a photo of me, dressed like 47, for the cover image of this book. Some of the features of the first game were vague little foreshadowing hints of what was to come, when the franchise finally produced the re-imagined not-really-a-sequel game, Hitman, sixteen years after Hitman: Codename 47 was released.

I can't tie MAME to one particular year, or any specific chapter of my life, so I'll take a break from the chronological journey and say a few things right here and now about it. In the beginning, when I first found MAME while I was searching the internet for old arcade games, I didn't believe it could be what it claimed to be, or do what it claimed to do. It sounded too good to be true, and I already knew that something that sounds too good to be true almost always turns out to be exactly that.

But MAME did do what it claimed to do, with no hidden catch, no malware, no adverts, no microtransactions. I remember phoning Sadboy to tell him I had Mr Do! on my PC, not a remake or a crap copy, but the original arcade game, running on an emulator. He couldn't believe it, the same way I hadn't believed it until I saw it. Mr Do! running flawlessly on my PC was mind-blowing, but it was only a tiny part of the MAME miracle. Now I could play Asteroids, my all-time favourite game from the Golden Age, and Space Invaders, Lunar Rescue, Frogger, Donkey Kong, an entire library of classic arcade games.

Some of those games didn't work properly, with incorrect colour palettes or missing sound samples, but none of that mattered. These were the original games, so all the old skills and tricks worked the same way they'd worked back in the Garway Moon, in Round Ear Records, and on the pier at Weston.

It wasn't just a technical emulation of old arcade games, it was a DOS-prompt command-line time machine transporting us back to the dawn of the Golden Age. Memories, long-forgotten quotes, the way we'd felt when we pumped 10p into one of those games for the first time; we were reliving history, playing games we thought we'd lost forever and already grieved over.

MAME gave the games and the Golden Age memories back to us, in a dodgy, black-market, illegal kind of way, but it felt righteous, it felt too good to be wrong. Some of the old video game companies had gone bust, disappeared forever, and there was no way their games would ever come back without an emulation project like MAME. Other companies were still around, like Atari and Nintendo, but they weren't releasing perfectly emulated versions of their old arcade games for the PC. Microsoft Arcade was good while it lasted, but the games in that compilation weren't perfect emulations, they were slightly different versions of the originals.

Playing old games on MAME wasn't a cheapskate alternative method of playing original eighties arcade games, it was the only way we could do it. I assured myself I'd spent enough 10p coins on those games in the past to more than justify playing them for free over a decade after they vanished from my life.

My inner philanthropist appreciated the opportunity MAME was giving to young kids who never had the chance to play any of the old arcade games the first time around. Posting YouTube videos of your little brother smashing his PlayStation because someone killed him in Fortnite is a totally valid way to spend your time, but what's your Galaxian high score? Three? And, no, I'm not accepting the rebuttal "That game is trash" as justification for living in ignorance of video game history. People playing Pokemon Go and claiming it gets them out of the house for a walk most likely haven't ever had to walk to the village pub in the pouring rain to play Space Invaders on a Sunday afternoon.

I'm lucky I've got diverse video gaming memories that aren't exclusively of me, sitting on the sofa, shouting at a TV screen. I have a weird kind of sympathy, not pity, for the kids who missed out on the Golden Age; it came and went in a few years, and if you weren't there, you'll never know how amazing it was. MAME can help, but an emulator time machine will only let you relive the memories you've already got.

Meanwhile, back in the first year of the twenty-first century, eight months without any income was starting to worry me. Long daily gym sessions were great, unlimited gaming time was also rather nice, but I hadn't expected to be out of work for that long.

Every week at the Dum rehearsal, Ade would ask me if I had a job yet and I'd say no. He was still working, somehow managing to have held onto a contract despite the post-millennium trend of cutbacks. One day in August, at a midweek Dum rehearsal, Ade told me he'd heard about a local mainframe programming job being advertised that matched my set of twentieth-century dinosaur skills. There was only one problem: it was a permanent job, not a contract.

I knew I didn't have a choice, I couldn't be picky, but I'd spent the last five years in an alternative employment universe of contracting, and I'd promised myself I'd never go back to a permie role. I contacted the agency advertising the job and I told them to get me an interview. The kid I talked to at the agency was the same as all the other kids at every other agency, a wind-up toy robot chirping a pre-programmed stream of blah-blah going-forwards corporate platitudes. "Just get me an interview," I said. "I'll get the job." It wasn't arrogance, just logic; I had all the technical skills they were asking for, and I'd been selling those skills at a premium rate for the last five years. Okay, it was arrogance. You got me.

I was interviewed by a lanky bloke dressed like a farmer at a wedding and a grumpy woman with an aggressive haircut. They offered me the job and I said thanks very much. On my second day in the new job, I told my manager they'd given me the wrong job, an analyst role, instead of the programming job I'd been offered at the interview. He told me there was a new analyst in another team, complaining because he didn't want to be a programmer. They'd managed to swap us around and put us both in the wrong job. A day later it was sorted out, and I was part of the mainframe support team, but I wasn't exactly overwhelmed with confidence for my new employers.

Diablo 2 had Hardcore mode. It was the first game I'd seen where the player could opt for a permadeath mode where many hours of progress could potentially be lost, a mode where the 'Game Over - start again' principle of early, 10p-a-go arcade games was being applied to a role-playing game with a single-player campaign that could take well over forty hours to complete. The way hardcore mode works out in all the games I've played is this: you almost always play in standard mode until you get familiar with the game, then you start a hardcore character, you play extremely cautiously for a while, you get overconfident in late game, you screw up in a predictably stupid way, your hardcore character dies and you lose all your loot and umpteen hours of gameplay.

This happened to me in Diablo 2 when I got a bit cocky in the third act and had my overconfidence smacked down by several witch doctors and their fireballs. There was no way to quickly quit out of Diablo 2 if you got into a bad situation because quitting initiated a disconnection countdown, you didn't immediately leave the game. Even yanking the mains plug out of the wall wouldn't save you.

That hardcore death in Diablo 2's third act put me off playing hardcore mode in any game for a few years. I still remember how I felt immediately after the Game Over message appeared on the screen, and it wasn't nice. I didn't feel angry, didn't want to throw my keyboard at the wall or smash my mouse with a hammer, I just felt empty, and stupid.

Hardcore mode teaches you a bunch of valuable life lessons such as caution, restraint, patience, always level up beyond the next area you're going into, don't start a fight unless you are absolutely sure you will win, run away whenever you suspect things might possibly go even slightly awry, and, most importantly: don't play Hardcore mode.

The first Hitman game was a bit of a hardcore, all-or-nothing game, where you frequently ended up restarting a level or loading a saved game if you made the most trivial mistake, but that was the whole point of the game, and you didn't lose hours and hours of progress when it happened.

On the other side of the fence, there was The Sims. It got so much hype before it came out, all the magazines printing pre-release articles about next-gen AI, emergent gameplay and infinite replayability; everyone was suckered into believing it was going to be worth playing, even me. It wasn't even a video game. That's the only excuse I can give it. It didn't matter how hard I tried to like The Sims, it was irredeemably bad. People tried to tell me it was fun because it let you wall a Sim character up in a small room with no food or water. Not fun. And only not fun for a minute or two. Playing The Sims was like shoving your head inside a doll's house and shouting in a foreign language you didn't understand. Only a lot less fun.

"But you can get a Sim job and marry a same-sex Sim," people said, as if this was what video games were supposed to be like in the new century. "And you can put Sim furniture in your Sim house. That's brilliant!"

No, that's not brilliant. That's a cruel and unusual punishment for being a gamer. Space Invaders was a video game. Doom was a video game. Diablo 2 was a video game. The Sims was a gullibility test. The emperor's new Tamagotchi. Oh look, I can see the emergent gameplay. No. You cannot see it. It does not exist. This isn't hindsight; I hated The Sims from day one, but I couldn't just ignore it and pretend it didn't exist, because it was too much of a threat. If I'd enjoyed playing it, I would have been happy. When it came out, everyone said it was the future of gaming. I thought if this is the future of gaming, I'm going to go back to blowing up rubbish bins with homemade bombs. Rubbish bins jammed full of copies of The Sims.

In September 2000, not long after I started in my new job, there were protests about the tax on fuel, including blockades that caused a short-term fuel shortage across the UK. This was generally a bad thing, particularly if you happened to own a 5.7 litre Chevrolet Camaro, had just started a new job, and drove a seventy-mile round trip to work every day.

Petrol stations everywhere had massive queues and they

were rationing the amount of fuel everyone could buy, which again was a pain in the neck if your car did about fifteen miles per gallon on a good day. As soon as the panic was over, I sold the Camaro and started driving around in a dull but grimly sensible Nissan Primera. A bloke from Scotland bought the Camaro. He came down to Hereford on a train, I met him at the train station and swapped my car for a bank draft he brought with him. He jumped in the Camaro and drove it back to Scotland, which probably cost him the same in petrol as he'd just paid for the car.

The first notable PC game release of 2001 was Black and White. I didn't like it. The Sims had started a trend of over-hyped games that didn't seem to be proper games, but everyone bought them anyway and some people got excited about random aspects of the sound, or the graphics, or the control methods, or, in the case of Black and White, a song the NPCs sang on a ship. The only good thing about novelty games was they were a novelty, so they didn't hang around very long. I only remember Black and White because of the fuss everyone made about it. As a game, it wasn't particularly memorable.

In my new job, it didn't take long for me to seek out and interact with other gamers. By then, I'd bought a PS2 but I wasn't using it anywhere near as much as my PC. Ico was probably the best PS2 game to come out in 2001. I bought Gran Turismo 3, hoping it would be better than GT2, but it wasn't.

One of the first games I talked about a lot at work was

Max Payne. I don't know why it had those annoying dream sequences, they spoiled the rest of the game for me, but the 'bullet time' slow-mo was great fun.

Return to Castle Wolfenstein wasn't bad, and there was a tough, glitchy open-world (sort of) RPG called Gothic which kept me entertained for a few hours but, overall, 2001 was noticeably short of decent PC games compared to the overload of the previous year.

I was off work with a flu virus the second week of September 2001. On the Tuesday, I was lying on the sofa under a blanket, shivering and sweating, watching daytime TV when the programme was interrupted with a news bulletin. A plane had crashed into the World Trade Centre. The news footage was all over the place, shaky long-shots of smoke, dust, chaos on the streets, people shouting, nobody really knowing what was going on. While I watched, a second plane crashed and the reporters were saying random things about horrifying coincidences, wildly estimating the number of dead and the risks the emergency services were taking. In the aftermath, one of the weirdest things I remember was Microsoft Flight Simulator being changed to remove the World Trade Centre amid media claims the terrorists used the flight sim to rehearse their attacks. I suppose they couldn't blame Judas Priest that time, so they had to try to blame video games.

2002 was a much better year than its predecessor as far as quality video game releases were concerned. I'm including Grand Theft Auto 3 in my list of 2002 games because that was the year it was released on the PC. I know it came out in October 2001 on the PS2, and I did play it on the PS2, but I played it much more on the PC, and I preferred aiming and sniping using a mouse, rather than a thumbstick controller, so in my gaming memories GTA3 was a 2002 game.

Other memorable 2002 releases included some all-time classics, some life-changing multiplayer games, and some complete crap (mostly on the PS2). Look at this bunch of PC games released in 2002: Hitman 2: Silent Assassin, Tom Clancy's Splinter Cell, Medal of Honor: Allied Assault, Battlefield 1942, Mafia, Age of Mythology, The Elder Scrolls 3: Morrowind, Neverwinter Nights, The Thing, Dungeon Siege, Medieval: Total War, Warcraft 3: Reign of Chaos, RollerCoaster Tycoon 2, and Unreal Tournament 2003.

The Hitman sequel was a big improvement over the first game, more consistently fun to play, definitely a must-have if you were into stealth games, although it wasn't so much a stealth game as a hide-in-plain-sight game due to the disguises. The developers seemed to have listened to all the criticisms of the first game, fixing most of the things that annoyed people or just didn't work very well. Overall, Hitman 2 was a lot of fun, and it even caused controversy and had to have a whole level removed, exactly the kind of publicity that never hurts game sales.

Splinter Cell was a proper stealth game that felt very different from Hitman, although they shared the basic principles of infiltration, remaining undetected and shooting people in the head with silenced pistols.

Medal of Honor was one of the first multiplayer games I played online. Someone from work hosted the games one week-night every week, mostly deathmatch or team deathmatch, and a group of us would join at an agreed time in the evening. I was on a dial-up modem connection, until I moved to live in Gloucester in October 2003, so I had to contend with laggy gameplay and rubber-banding most of the time. It was still a good laugh, that perfect entertainment combo of World War 2 and throwing hand grenades at your co-workers.

The day after a Medal of Honor session, we always had a big discussion or a series of big discussions about it in work. Kill counts would be ridiculed, tactics would be dismantled, and the inappropriate close-range use of bazookas and Panzerfausts would be deemed 'lame', not in the spirit of a realistic re-enactment of World War 2. At the time, my online Medal of Honor character was called Johnny Napalm. When confronted with the accusation of lameness and stupidity for the reckless use of a Panzerfaust inside a building I changed my online name to Evil Johnny Napalm, explaining that I was role-playing a crazy person who had no regard for self-preservation or the rules of war. Bizarrely, that sorted the problem out. The single-player Medal of Honor game was excellent, the D-day landing level being one of the most memorable (and difficult) of any first-person shooter I've ever played.

Mafia was an interesting game, with a ridiculously difficult early-game car race that has attained notoriety not only for being frustratingly hard but also for not really fitting in with the rest of the gangster-crime gameplay. I eventually completed the race after being seriously tempted to give up the game completely, promising myself I would definitely quit if there was another race later in the game. There wasn't, and they even patched the game to make the original race an optional event that could be skipped due to all the negative criticism it received.

Age of Mythology was a sequel to Age of Empires, but with a theme of mythical heroes and monsters instead of straightforward armies and castles. As a big fan of Ray Harryhausen films like Jason and the Argonauts, the whole mythological theme really appealed to me, even though real-time strategy has never been one of my favourite genres.

The first two Elder Scrolls games used the same type of technical tricks to give the impression the player was in a huge open world. The third Elder Scrolls game, Morrowind, used a totally new game engine and simulated a smaller, but far more detailed and genuinely open world. The landscape was a weird environment of volcanic rocks and giant mushrooms. The main quest could be permanently broken if certain NPCs were killed, and it was possible to level your character up into a virtually unkillable superhero with godlike powers. All of this was quite astonishing in 2002, and Morrowind is quite rightly remembered with respect and adoration by the majority of players who had the good fortune to spend many, many hours in it.

The movie tie-in game of The Thing is fascinating for a

couple of different reasons: it came out twenty years after the film's theatrical release, and it's a really good game, one of the best film tie-ins of all time. Why is it so good? It stays true to the source material, it also includes locations, characters and events from the original film. The survival elements are mostly basic environmental hazards: it's cold enough to kill you if you wander about outside for too long, and fire can burn you. There's a fairly simple 'trust' feature, where your actions and the current situation can alter the level of trust your team members have for you. Giving someone a gun can raise their trust level, but do you trust them enough to give them a gun?

Meanwhile, mutant alien creatures of various sizes and abilities are constantly jump-scaring everyone while trying to bite your head off. The Thing is a hard game, veering close to painfully frustrating at times but always good enough to keep you battling on to the end. The only complaint I had back in 2002 was you didn't play as Kurt Russell's character from the film. It would have been amazing if they could have got him to fully voice-act the main character; the game would have been a much bigger deal, and a much bigger seller.

Chapter 11
Musical Interlude Three
'I can't see beyond yesterday.'

The first proper gig Dum played was on stage in a big pub called The Kerry in Hereford, early in 2001. We'd already played at a party in a sports hall, but that was more of a glorified rehearsal in front of an audience who knew us and weren't going to bottle us off for being rubbish. We played everything too fast at the party, which was mostly my fault due to being hyped up on excitement, and I promised I wouldn't do it again.

The Kerry gig went well, considering we were completely unknown and playing a set of mostly original songs in front of an audience who didn't know us. At least I didn't play everything too fast that time.

We were rehearsing once a week at the studio in Cheltenham, writing new songs and improving existing ones, making a lot of noise and having a great time. I'd leave work, drive across to Ade's house on the opposite side of Gloucester, shove my gear into the back of his estate car, and he'd drive us to Cheltenham to meet Joel at the rehearsal studio.

Joel had a graphic design job so he could print decent flyers and posters to advertise our gigs. The first local gig we played was in Cheltenham at a pub called The Fish and Fiddle. I stuck some of Joel's gig promo flyers up in work and spent a couple of weeks asking everyone I knew if they could come along and give us some support. It worked out well, much better than I'd expected. Most people tend to say they'll come and watch your band play when you ask them, but on the day they realise they had a haircut appointment, or their dog had to go to the vet, or they forgot, or there was a really good episode of Eastenders on, or whatever. But most of the people who said they'd go to see Dum at The Fish and Fiddle turned up like they said they would.

Sadboy and his wife drove over from the other side of Ross-on-Wye with a couple of friends, loads of people from work turned up, and there were quite a few pub regulars too, so it was a pretty big crowd for a relatively unknown band's first local gig. We were the only band playing so we put every song we knew in the set, including covers of 'Breed' (Nirvana) and 'Ace of Spades' (Motorhead). We even included Joel's silly song about the joys of driving, 'Turn your lights on', which ended up being the one everyone remembered, probably because it was the one with the most swearing in the chorus. By this point, Ade had resigned himself to the fact he was the singer as well as the guitarist, and he put a lot of effort into practising how to sing in tune and also sound like a punk-band vocalist. He did a great job of it, way better than I would have done. I still did backing shouting on songs like

'Sex, Drugs and Pokemon' and 'They Say', and I did the majority of the mic-chat between songs when we played live.

Before every gig I always felt sick, or I spent half an hour in the toilet with dodgy guts, but as soon as I was behind the microphone with my bass slung over my shoulder I just went for it, shouting out whatever stupid nonsense came into my head at the time, often bad-taste opinion on such diverse topics as suicide bombers and Craig David.

When we'd finished our set at the Fish and Fiddle, people from work came up to me with that look on their faces they get when you turn into someone else right in front of them and they don't know which version is you. The next day at work, one of them told me they were surprised to see me doing what I did, shouting and jumping about, playing the bass, being in a punk band. They'd only seen me sitting at a desk in the office, writing programs on the mainframe, so that's who they thought I was. And most of the day, Monday to Friday, that is who I was, otherwise nobody would have paid me to be there, would they?

The three main places we played in Cheltenham were the Fish and Fiddle, The Two Pigs, and The Slug and Lettuce. Sometimes we'd be the only band playing, other times we'd be the support act for another band, and on rare occasions we'd be the main band, or there'd be several bands on and we'd only be given enough time to play a few songs.

I set up a Dum website, the one with the 'What's the most important thing in life?' question on it, and Ade found a rehearsal shed close to where he lived which saved us time not having to drive to and from Cheltenham on practice days. One of his neighbours owned the shed, a warehouse full of random building materials and bags of potatoes, and he let us practice in there for free. Some days, we'd turn up and there would be so much stuff cluttering the place up we'd spend half an hour carefully rearranging it so we could fit the drum kit and all our other gear in there. The acoustics weren't too bad in the shed, good enough that we recorded the drums in there for some of the tracks on our self-produced 'May Cause Drowsiness' album.

At one of the gigs in The Two Pigs there was hardly anyone there, and the few people who turned up were just sitting at the bar paying no attention to us. I didn't care, I remembered what Henry Rollins had written about situations like that, when you play as hard to an empty room as you'd play to a packed venue full of fans.

We made a few different intro recordings to play at the start of gigs. I put sound samples on there from TV shows like Captain Scarlet and Dr Who, and sound effects like sirens and bombs exploding and the 20th Century Fox fanfare. We started a lot of gigs playing a cover of the theme music from Buffy the Vampire Slayer, going straight out of that into 'Smile' via an extended bit of guitar feedback. We started some gigs with 'They Say' because it was one of our shorter, faster songs and it had enough swearing in it to wake the audience up. Or the empty room.

People would sometimes ask me what our songs were about, but we didn't have any kind of overall lyrical theme and the individual songs were not exactly deep and meaningful. 'B-Movies' was one I wrote, not much more than a list of subtle and not-so-subtle film and TV references. I thought it was clever, and it had one rather convoluted line in it that Ade had trouble singing but I refused to change because it was funny watching him singing it live: 'Some teenage chick, piloting an interstellar hyperdrive ship'.

I was getting a coffee out of a vending machine in work when one of the young women from the IT Security team came up to me and said, "You're in a band, aren't you?" I thought it was cool, she wasn't exactly playing hard to get, and it's a nice story to tell when someone asks me how I met my wife. I probably said something dumb when she asked, but I like to think I said, "Damn right I'm in a band, you should come see us some time. I can get you a backstage pass."

When she did come to see us, she didn't like the music we played; she was into pop music like Take That and Steps.

RollerCoaster Tycoon 2 came out in October 2002. I played it a lot, to the point where it not only interfered with my bass practice but also my Buffy watching schedule. One of the best money-making rides was a metal coaster track with a powered launch. You didn't have to make a complete circuit, so you could have the powered launch going straight into a loop, a photo section immediately after that, followed by a steep, almost vertical section of track where the coaster train would go all the way up, then gravity would take it back down, back around the loop and into the station section. The combination of high ride excitement, short duration, low construction cost and small land area needed made this a brilliant profit generator. That was one of the reasons RCT2 was so much fun, you could try out all sorts of daft ideas or you could pick prefabricated rides from a massive list and concentrate on making a park that looked really cool with lakes and hedges, and paved paths that spelled out swear words when you zoomed the view out far enough to see it all.

You could create a coaster with really high G-forces and rename it Super-Puke or Mega-Hurl, then build stalls selling burgers, ice cream, and candy floss right next to it and watch all the park guests throwing up as soon as they came off the ride. The scenario challenges were fine, but the real fun of the game was the sandbox environment with its sense of unlimited freedom to experiment and build crazy rides.

A year after RCT2 was released, in fact almost exactly a year later in October 2003, I went to Las Vegas and ate a load of ice cream before going on the Speed coaster at the Nascar Café. It was one of those powered launch rides with a loop into a vertical section of track, with gravity taking the train backwards to the station, just like the money-makers I liked to build in RCT2. I was the only person on it at the time and, yes, I felt sick for hours afterwards.

Another life-changing game came out in October 2002, and that was Unreal Tournament 2003. It immediately became a regular weekly kill-fest for the gamers at work and it sticks in my mind as one of the best online games I've ever played. I called my UT2003 character Dead John, which seemed funny at the time, and my favourite game mode was always Capture the flag.

The quantity of important video game releases didn't diminish in 2003. Call of Duty came out, giving us yet another online multiplayer deathmatch game where players could be yelled at and accused of being lame idiots following the inappropriate use of bazookas in enclosed spaces. I'm trying to imagine how we must have felt playing Call of Duty when it was the first game to be called that, and not the umpteenth version of the same game with a battle royale mode tacked on just because it was trendy and fashionable.

Manhunt was wholesome fun for the family, you could suffocate people with plastic bags and beat them to death with hammers. Game developers in the early 2000s must have been actively trying to get their releases banned by including content guaranteed to annoy the hand-wringing "Ban this sick filth" crowd. Manhunt went further than most games in its quest to be labelled vile and disturbing. In the UK, Game and Dixons stopped selling Manhunt after it was linked to a murder case where a copy of the game was found in the killer's house. The media didn't mention all the copies of The Sims games and 'Now that's what I call music' compilations also found in his house. I played Manhunt, but it became frustratingly tedious after a while with its time limits and frankly punitive gameplay.

Star Wars - Knights of the Old Republic gave us a deep, complex role-playing game in an early incarnation of the Star Wars universe. The only problem I had with the game was the amount of time I would have had to devote to it in order to make a significant amount of progress. By the time it came out, October 2003, I was starting to develop worrying domestic tendencies such as moving into a house with my girlfriend, buying a new kitchen, choosing new sofas, pretty much all the things they'd wanted me to do in The Sims.

Halfway through June 2003, on a Saturday evening, I drove from my girlfriend's house to Tesco on my own to get some food. I was pushing the trolley around the aisles, dodging through the capacity crowd you always get in supermarkets on a Saturday evening, when my phone rang. I thought it was probably my girlfriend adding a late item to the shopping list, but it wasn't. It was Ade's wife, Amanda. "I've been trying to call you for hours," she said. "Adrian is dead."

She told me they'd been sitting in a coffee shop in Cheltenham, everything had been fine and then it wasn't. Ade started having trouble breathing and a few minutes later he was dead. She didn't know what had happened. I can't remember what I said to her. I went to the checkout and paid for the shopping, carried the bag back to my car and sat in the driver's seat staring out of the windscreen at a normal car park on a normal Saturday evening.

I phoned Joel while I was sitting in the car; he already knew about Ade and he sounded completely broken. I don't remember what I said to him. I had a CD of Dum songs in the car, so I put it on and sat there listening to Ade playing the guitar and singing, then I drove back to my girlfriend's house listening to Dum all the way.

She opened the front door and I stood there holding the shopping bag. "Amanda phoned here, trying to get in touch with you," she said. "She sounded upset. Has something happened?"

I said, "He's fucking dead," and I started crying.

In the week after, I went to see Amanda. She'd stopped eating, and she was focusing completely on organising Ade's funeral and everything else that had to be done. She told me about all the people who were going to speak at the funeral, and a couple of Ade's friends who were going to be playing acoustic guitars during the service. She told me she wanted me to be the first to get up and speak at the funeral.

I said I'd do it. I tried to figure out how I should be feeling, how I was going to deal with standing up and talking at the start of the funeral service, but any thoughts I had about it felt like I was being selfish. My friends didn't know what to say to me, it was like a circle of nobody knowing what to say to anyone else.

I went to work, to the gym, and I played video games; everything was normal apart from my friend was dead and I didn't know how to deal with it. I changed my character name in Unreal Tournament 2003 from Dead John to Admiral Browning; I didn't want to be playing a character with the word 'Dead' in the name, it just felt completely wrong.

One of Dum's songs was called 'Just another pop star'. I wrote the lyrics for that one, and there's a line in the song that goes 'Didn't see it coming, couldn't have known, dropped stone dead on his mobile phone' and I've always regretted writing that now, like I was predicting the future with a song lyric.

I told my manager at work that I was going to my friend's funeral and his reaction was to tell me I had to take it as annual leave or make the hours up to cover the time I was out of the office. That's how much some people care when they have to decide between behaving like a decent human being or following the corporate rule-book to the letter. He was a vindictive twat all round, he tried to get me demoted during a company grade reshuffle a couple of years later but I fought it and I won. Not that it was difficult, obviously. What's that put-down, the one about avoiding a battle of wits because I wouldn't want to fight an unarmed man? Yeah, that would be the one, but I don't avoid those fights, I like easy wins. Imagine being such a thoughtless, ignorant prick that you're only remembered for being just that by a bloke writing an autobiography about video games. That has to suck.

I booked the day off as annual leave and I went to the funeral with my girlfriend. I told her she didn't have to go, but she didn't want me to go to it on my own, without her.

The funeral was in the church in Hempsted, close to where Ade had lived. We went in and sat on a pew. The church was packed. Everyone looked shocked, or utterly miserable. Nobody was talking. Most people were crying. I had words printed on a sheet of paper, things I was planning to say when I stood up in front of everyone. I kept thinking about people I knew who made a big fuss about being asked to be the best man at a wedding because they didn't want to stand up in front of a bunch of people they didn't know and try to tell some jokes and do a speech. I've never been asked to be anyone's best man, I'm guessing it would be a total breeze compared to doing the opening speech at a friend's funeral.

Ade had been thirty-five when he died. His coffin was at the front, where everyone could see it from the pews. I looked at what I'd written, it was blurred and pointless. All I could hear was people crying. The blokes playing acoustic guitars looked like they were crying while they played. I couldn't imagine a worse situation. I got up and went to stand at the front of the church, with Ade's coffin on my left and Joel standing on my right.

The church was full, everyone was beyond sad. Some people were looking at me but there was no anticipation on anyone's face, they were just sitting there feeling awful. I kept looking at the coffin on one side of me, Joel on the other, the crowd of people in front of us. It was like the three of us were on stage again, one last time. I could feel the piece of paper in my hand, but it wasn't going to be any use. I thought about Ade, all the gigs we'd played, the way I always felt before a gig, like I was going to puke, and then getting up on stage and shouting whatever stupid thing came into my head.

I looked at the sad, shocked faces, everyone waiting for me to start saying something that wouldn't make any difference anyway. If I'd tried to read the words off the paper, I would have choked and started crying. I closed my right hand into a fist, raised my arm. "Hello Hempsted!" like we were playing a stadium, which would never happen, not now, not ever.

The whole church seemed to sigh, some sense of relief. I hadn't made anything better, nothing could make it better, but I changed it enough. I could see Joel nodding his head, knowing I'd done the right thing. Amanda was looking at me, crying but with a gleam of gratitude in her eyes. She came up to me after, when it was all over, and she said, "That was fucking brilliant." And she never swore, didn't like the Dum songs with swearing in them.

After I did that out-of-place but totally necessary intro, I said some things about the three of us, me and Joel and Ade, and the band, and I read a few lines of a Dum song that were on the piece of paper. Ade would have thought I did okay, but he would have preferred to still be alive.

Whenever I hear a new band that Ade would have liked, I wish he could still be around so I could tell him about it, but he was always the one who knew about the cool new bands before I did. I still miss him, and Dum never got to be as good as we were going to be.

Not long after the funeral, I told my girlfriend I wasn't scared of flying any more. I said I wanted to go to Las Vegas, it sounded like the kind of crazy place I was always meant to go.

Here are the lyrics to 'Addicted', the song Ade liked enough for me to read it at his funeral.

I can't be angry any more
I've got nothing to quit
Can't get addicted

I can't see beyond yesterday
I've got nothing to say
And you won't listen, listen anyway

Chapter 12

I promise I won't spawn-camp
'Wake up, Mr. Freeman. Wake up,
and smell the ashes.'

2004 was another massive year for PC games. Check this list out: World of Warcraft, The Chronicles of Riddick: Escape from Butcher Bay, Unreal Tournament 2004, Sacred, Far Cry, Hitman Contracts, Thief: Deadly Shadows, Joint Operations: Typhoon Rising, Doom 3, Rome: Total War, Half-Life 2, Vampire The Masquerade - Bloodlines. And those were just some of the good ones.

By now, I'd moved into a house in Gloucester with my girlfriend, and I finally had broadband internet access instead of the dial-up modem connection I'd been struggling with for the last few years.

There was a regular group of gamers at work playing most of the online multiplayer games. One or two of them only liked first-person shooters, and we didn't all play every game that came out. I got the initial subscription for World of Warcraft, I think it was for three months, and I didn't play it again after that ran out. When I was playing it, I was doing it all wrong, at least by the standards of the people who were playing it properly. Instead of questing, grinding and levelling up the way you're supposed to, I was doing things like seeing how far I could get into high-level areas by swimming along the coastline, or hanging around with a higher-level friend just to go sight-seeing in zones where I wouldn't have lasted more than ten seconds on my own.

I'd been playing a lot of video games with Ben, a good friend who was really into first-person shooters. He was obsessive about quest completions in RPGs but he was also constantly amused by the stupid things I did in games, like finding the highest climbable part of a game area and jumping off it. Ben ran a PDA website for a while, with hardware and software reviews, and its own user forum. I bought a PDA because it was another portable gaming device and I was also using it to run sat-nav software as justification for owning it. I wrote some reviews for Ben's website, and I remember a few of the games being extremely good fun. Toki Tori was excellent, I'm not entirely sure how I missed it until I played it on a PDA. It was a puzzle platform game, with the emphasis on the puzzling rather than the platforming, and it had cute, detailed graphics.

I was on World of Warcraft with Ben one night, when Silky, a far more serious MMO player from work, was on there at the same time. All three of us were talking in game chat and we agreed to meet up in Stormwind, one of the cities in the game. Ben and I went into a building there and waited for Silky to come into the same room, then the two of us started jumping up and down on a bed. Silky's character was just standing there, I can only imagine he was staring at his monitor thinking *what the fuck are these idiots doing?* He probably thought we were going to team up and do a load of quests together, power-levelling or something else he would have considered to be a more appropriate way to spend time in WoW than jumping about on a bed.

The Riddick game was a surprise, because it was not only a decent film tie-in but a good game by anyone's standards. It had several cool features, such as a minimal HUD and an emphasis on melee combat and stealth. Like Hitman, it was another game where I could play as a bald psycho. No typecasting.

Sacred was one of many Diablo clones, not the best and not the worst, although arguably much better than its own sequel. It did a decent job of filling the action-RPG gap until a far superior action-RPG, Titan Quest, appeared in 2006.

Ben and I had been excited about Far Cry for ages before the full game was released. When the demo came out in January 2004 we played it relentlessly, although probably not as much as we played the pre-alpha demo of Stalker: Shadow of Chernobyl, but we still had another three years to wait for that game to be released.

Far Cry's open, tropical island setting was new and different at the time, and there was a great sense of freedom, at least in the outdoor areas. The game started inside a gloomy tunnel, much like any other first-person shooter, but as you made your way along it, you could see outside through holes in the walls. The sky was bright blue, as was the sea, and there was lush tropical foliage everywhere. When I went to Hawaii on our honeymoon in 2005 I bought a red-and-white Hawaiian shirt that looked just like the one worn by Jack Carver, the Far Cry protagonist.

There's not a lot to say about Half-Life 2 that hasn't already been said a million times before in magazines, gaming awards, and online. It was excellent, a real evolution for first-person shooters with marvellous physics-based puzzles and the Gravity Gun, one of the coolest and funniest weapons in any game ever.

It's funny these days (2019) to see all the gamer kiddies frothing and gibbering about Fortnite because it's the best game ever, with one hundred players on one island. Okay, great, now let's talk about a game we had fifteen years earlier, Joint Operations: Typhoon Rising, and its Escalation expansion pack. How about one hundred and fifty simultaneous players, multiple maps, multiple game modes, tanks, helicopters, motorbikes, parachutes, driving a jeep inside a transport chopper, driving an armoured car onto a transport boat... I think you get the idea. But I haven't finished. I need to froth and gibber some more.

Joint Operations was an amazing game, every kind of military combat carnage you could wish for. The best games were team deathmatches on a huge map with two big islands. You could load up a chopper and fly across to the enemy base, sail one of a variety of seagoing vessels across, or stay behind and shoot the crap out of invading enemies. There were remote-detonated C4 charges; those were hilarious. Sneak into an enemy base, drop a C4 charge inside one of the big transport choppers or behind a tank, hide and wait until someone on the enemy team gets into the vehicle, press the button and watch the furious comments appear in game chat.

I liked to take a sniper rifle, get in a rubber dinghy and go along the coast to the far side of an enemy base. I'd sit there, sniping the enemy players as they wandered about, or after they got into the pilot seat of a helicopter. They'd be typing abuse in game chat - 'LAME SNIPER STOP SPAWN CAMPING!' - and I'd keep doing it until one of them figured out where I was and stayed alive long enough to start shooting back at me.

Three blokes from work formed a Joint Ops clan with me, we called it SOG and it mostly stood for Sad Old Gits but it could have been anything else with those initial letters. My clan name was SOG-Yoda. One of the SOG group was Carl. He was a legend, he took gaming really seriously and he was good at Joint Ops. I was on there one day, trying to make a tower of tanks and armoured cars by hauling them into the air with a transport chopper and lowering them down one at a time on top of each other. Carl turned up and I thought he was going to just laugh and go off to shoot people, but after I told him what I was trying to do he really got into it and we spent ages stacking vehicles while the war went on around us.

Another time, Carl and I were on a team together on a small map and there were only a few people playing. The other team started putting messages in chat saying we should keep the fighting away from the bases so nobody got spawn-camped. We said, okay, no problem. A bit later, Carl got shot while he was in our base, and he completely lost it. He had a go at them in chat, then we went over and started shooting up their base. After they killed us, Carl told me to get in a jeep - one with a big mounted machine gun on the back - and he manned the gun while I drove into their base camp and went round and round in circles while Carl kept machine-gunning them every time they respawned. He was in chat the whole time, telling them it was their fault because they started it, until they got completely pissed off and left the game.

Compared to 2004, or in fact any of the previous years of the new century, 2005 was a mediocre year for PC game releases. There were some classic console games released in 2005, for example God of War and Shadow of the Colossus, but I'd sold my PS2 after leaving it unused for a few months so I didn't play many of the console games from the mid 2000s. There were a few decent PC games released in 2005 but mostly we were in a world of sequel overload. Some of the sequels were good games, but the age of the franchise cash-grab was here and it wasn't going to let originality and creativity get in the way of a quick profit.

Hitting every branch of the PC family tree on the way down in 2005 were: Call of Duty 2, GTA San Andreas, Need For Speed: Most Wanted, Civilisation IV, Zoo Tycoon 2, Age of Empires II, Quake 4, Serious Sam 2, Black and White 2, Myst V, Dungeon Siege 2, Worms 4, Battlefield 2, Star Wars KotOR 2, and SWAT 4.

While I wouldn't go as far as to claim the non-sequel games in 2005 were a hundred percent original, a couple of them were real gems, most memorably Guild Wars, an MMORPG that wasn't a life-draining grind-fest. Ben and I started playing Guild Wars at the same time. My first character was a warrior called Sheena Packer, Ben's character was called Simon Packer. The way Ben played RPGs was to stick with one character and do everything in the game with it, all the quests, all the exploring, and when everything was done he'd leave the game alone and find a new one to play. Depending on how much I was enjoying an RPG I might create loads of different characters to see what the unique class skills were like, or because I liked the early stages of a game where the levelling up was quick. Or I might spend ages just messing about, or trying to get some of the weirder achievements.

In Guild Wars, after I'd played through most of the content with the Sheena Packer character, I started to notice an in-game subculture where max-level characters were running groups of low level players across the map, specifically to hard-to-reach areas and most prolifically to Droknar's Forge, an area near the end of the game where the 'best armour in the game' could be obtained. One of the interesting features of Guild Wars was the absence of level restrictions on equipping armour. This meant, in theory, that a level one character could equip endgame armour. The catch, of course, was the area where the endgame armour could be obtained was so far through the game that a character would most likely have reached the level cap by the time they fought and quested their way there.

However, there was a shortcut through a ridiculously tough sequence of zones, pretty much impossible to fight through at any level and immensely time-consuming if you tried it. The solution, and it was an insanely genius exploitation of the game's skill-sets and party mechanics, was for one or two max-level characters - almost always Warriors with a secondary class of Monk, at least at first, before the expansions started coming out - to form a party with some low-level characters and run through the shortcut zones to the area with the endgame armour shops. I found out about this when I was playing on new characters, looking for ways to level up quickly and get through the game faster.

The Droknar's Forge runs started from a small location called Beacon's Perch, up in the snowy Shiverpeak Mountains zone. At any time when you'd be at Beacon's Perch, you'd see players announcing things like "Drok run 3k pay at Rankor" or "Looking for run to Droks will pay 5k", the latter usually being experienced players levelling alternative characters or, frequently enough to be annoying, muppets with no intention of paying but looking for a free ride in exchange for lies.

I paid to have a few low-level characters run to Droknar's Forge, and I noticed the runners were using Warrior/Monk characters, which was the same class combo as Sheena Packer. I asked a few of the runners about the skills they were using and one of them gave me the list and told me they'd take me on a test run once I'd acquired the skills needed for the running build. I had some of the skills already, and only one of the others was particularly hard to get.

In Guild Wars, some of the skills had to be obtained by using a Signet of Capture on a defeated enemy, usually unique elites or bosses in tough parts of the map. One of the essential running skills was 'Charge!', only available from an Abomination boss called Balthazaar's Cursed in the fire islands zone near the end of the game. It took a while, but I eventually got the 'Charge!' skill. I went to Beacon's Perch and met up with the runner who said they'd take me on a test run, and the training began.

The 'Charge!' skill increased the speed of any player within range for a short time, and then it had a cooldown period before it could be used again. If there were two runners, they could take turns using 'Charge!' so it was active almost all the time. That was the first thing to learn. There was a lot more.

Each of the three zones between Beacon's Perch and Camp Rankor had their own hazards. The first area had some giant worms bursting out of the ground, which needed carefully timed use of a skill that prevented knockdown. The next area had a few nasty sorcerer type enemies and ranged attackers that mostly just had to be totally avoided, and the third area was a meandering pass full of frost giants and massive griffons.

Every run was different because the enemy spawns were somewhat randomised. You might go out into the first area and get hit by two or three groups of magic users at the same time as the giant worms, usually a run-restart scenario unless you were really lucky. Other times, there might only be one group of wandering enemies nowhere near the worms and you'd breeze through it.

Anyone could conceivably have a character with a runner build, but doing the Droknar's run well enough to start making money as a human taxi-cab required a lot of practice. The route had to be learned and safe spots needed to be memorised until it was all second nature, and alternative Plan-B strategies had to be developed in the event of nightmare enemy spawns. I wanted to be a runner, so I listened to what I was told and I did a lot of solo test runs before I started touting for business at Beacon's Perch.

There was something raw and intriguing about going alone through the gateway from Beacon's into the first zone, Lornar's Pass, legging it through there, into Dreadnought's Drift, and then pausing on the far side of the portal into the third zone, Snake Dance, before trusting everything you knew and running straight through a crowd of griffons.

Getting to Camp Rankor wasn't the end of the Droknar's Forge run, but getting there meant your whole party would arrive, and they would all have it permanently unlocked as a fast-travel location. It was the place where most runners wanted to be paid, and where most scumbag passengers chose to leave the party without paying.

Once the party passengers had either paid up or been abused in global chat for not paying, the run continued through Talus Chute, the last zone before Droknar's Forge. It was generally taken for granted that the run was a success once you'd reached Camp Rankor, but I had a few runs through Talus that ended very badly due to crazy crowd spawns blocking the narrow trail at the start of the zone.

I bought all the Guild Wars expansion packs, and I ended up with a full roster of maxed-out characters with great gear, mostly funded by running players to Droknar's and other distant locations on the map. I quit playing and uninstalled the game forever when my account was hacked and all the gold and gear was removed. I never played Guild Wars again, and I didn't play the sequel because you learn as you gain experience, in life as in online role-playing games.

I got married in October 2005, at a wedding chapel in Las Vegas. The legal, form-signing part of the wedding was at a post office where we queued to see a cashier for twenty minutes, my wife-to-be in her wedding dress and both of us laughing at how surreal it was. The wedding chapel had a sign above the door outside, saying it was the chapel where Jon Bon Jovi got married. The service at the chapel wasn't as tacky as we thought it was going to be, and the weather in Vegas was perfect for wedding photos. When we went back to the Bellagio, there was a bloke playing the piano in one of the bar areas and he stopped playing whatever he was playing and went straight into the wedding march as we walked past. That really made my wife's day, and it also made up for me being banned from having an Elvis impersonator at the wedding.

From Vegas, we went to Hawaii for a few days for our

honeymoon and I got the worst sunburn ever while I was on Waikiki beach. I've been a fan and advocate of factor-fifty sunblock ever since.

After the comatose flatline of gaming sequels in 2005, 2006 gave us some serious defibrillator-induced spikes with games like Oblivion, the next chapter in the Elder Scrolls series (not actually a sequel, before you say anything), Hitman: Blood Money (an evolutionary leap rather than a sequel, before you even think of saying anything), and Titan Quest (this one was not a sequel, but definitely a Diablo clone).

I played Oblivion a lot, certainly more than I'd played Morrowind and I'd racked up hundreds of hours on that one. Oblivion was the first single-player RPG where doing the main questline wasn't as much fun as wandering about exploring and finding strange side quests, the majority of which were far more entertaining than picking up yet another main quest involving going through a demonic portal into the tedious Oblivion dimension. Oblivion was the first game in the Elder Scrolls series to have an arena, the only one to date because Skyrim hasn't got one unless you add it with a mod. You could battle your way to the top of the arena fight club or just bet on the fights if you were too much of a wuss to participate.

Ten years earlier, the arena from Oblivion could have been an entire game on its own; in Oblivion it was one small, optional part of a huge, ambitious game. Ignoring the main quest, which I did after I'd completed it once on my first character, there was an absolute ton of stuff to see and do in Oblivion. The Daedric artefacts were back again, mostly the same types of item that had appeared in the first Elder Scrolls game but with their own unique quests to obtain them now instead of identikit fetch quests in randomly generated dungeons. The Dark Brotherhood was a completely optional faction, but also one of the really fun questlines in Oblivion. Getting into the DB wasn't too difficult, and could be achieved quickly on a new character once you knew what had to be done.

Character class selection and skill choice was opened up, ostensibly to allow players to freely play the game however they wanted, and to be whatever type of character they wanted to be. The reality of this open choice in an open world was that it was really easy to get yourself into a right mess, where non-combat skills levelled your character up, the majority of enemies scaled to your level, and you got royally whupped by every bad guy you were unlucky enough to meet. The skill-levelling system could be exploited, for example by not including stealth in your primary or secondary skills, and then levelling stealth up by crouching in a dark corner of a populated room, turning auto-run on, and going off to watch a film or do some shopping for a few hours while your stealth skill levelled up. Your character would stay at level one, while stealth maxed out. It was slow, an arguably pointless process, but the game's skill mechanics allowed you to do it so it was a viable tactic. At least once, anyway, if only to see what would happen.

Oblivion used the same kind of 'escape from a dungeon' game start as Arena had, but this time it was more of a tutorial sequence than just being dumped into a dungeon and left to fend for yourself. And you had Patrick Stewart with you, at least for a few minutes, so there was a sense of Shakespearean gravitas to go with the glitchy sword-swinging and plasticine NPC faces.

Titan Quest and Oblivion were both RPGs, and they were released within the space of a few months of each other in 2006, but they were very different games. Titan Quest was very much the illegitimate child of Diablo, one of many games lumped together under the casual stereotype of 'Diablo clone', but it took the action RPG blueprint and did a lot more with it than simply churning out yet another lacklustre imitation of Blizzard's original game. The mythological theme was nothing new, but Titan Quest made it look amazing. Instead of procedurally generated areas, Titan Quest had unique, hand-crafted pastures, forests, coastlines and cities. It was split into three (before any expansion packs) distinct story zones: Ancient Greece, Egypt, and China.

Many of the enemies in each area were different, for example there were centaurs and gorgons in Greece, giant scarab beetles and scorpions in Egypt, and an army of terracotta soldiers in China, as well as sabre-tooth cats, raptors, and yetis. The game basics were familiar for anyone who'd played Diablo or Diablo 2: kill enemies, collect loot, level up, repeat, while travelling along a fairly linear route through the game. There was a story, but it was more of an unessential explanation of what was happening than an emotional motivation to continue the journey. Something bad is happening, monsters are everywhere, someone needs to go kill 'em all ... over to you, Player One. You know the drill.

Titan Quest didn't have a hardcore mode, but I still played it with an obsessive desire to keep each character's death count at zero, with varying degrees of success. I also tried a couple of alternative ways of playing after completing all the standard content on several different characters. I decided to see how far I could travel across the map without killing a single enemy while also keeping the player death count at zero. There were counters for both those statistics, so keeping track of it was easy. I knew there was a point I wouldn't be able to pass, halfway through Greece, where a trio of Gorgons had to be killed in order to progress beyond a locked door in a cave. There was no other way to get past, but the Gorgon cave was so far from the start of the game, getting there without dying or killing anything seemed extremely unlikely.

I had an initial attempt which ended badly, but I figured out a few things that hadn't previously occurred to me. There were areas where friendly NPCs were fighting enemies, and the enemies dropped loot when they were killed, no matter whether they were killed by the player or a friendly NPC. Some of the random loot drops were very nice, occasionally rare green and even epic blue items. Without killing anything, the character would be too low level to equip the really good items, but they could be sold to traders, the money then used to buy decent white-rated armour with lower requirements for character level and strength. There was always a big fight going on near a Spartan military camp which had its own player spawn point, so I passively farmed the hell out of it by loading the game at that spawn point, waiting for the nearby fight to run its course, looting everything that dropped, equipping or selling the looted gear, quitting, going back in and doing it all over again. A few hundred times.

I also figured out something that should have been obvious: some quests could be completed without killing anything. Not many, but enough to get a new character to level three before reaching the Gorgon cave. Those two levelups meant a mastery (character class) could be chosen, and some points could be put into a skill or two to boost the survivability of the otherwise feeble character. For example, in the Defence mastery there's a skill that lowers the strength requirement for armour, extremely useful if you're never going higher than level three, and putting points into the mastery bar will permanently increase a character's health.

Using a combination of cowardly post-skirmish looting, and heroically completing quests that didn't involve fighting, the best I managed was to reach the impassable Gorgon cave with a level three character who had suffered zero deaths and killed zero enemies. It's a shame they put that 'must kill to continue' point in the game, but then I doubt the developers ever considered that someone might be daft enough to try running all the way through Greece without killing anything.

One of the features of Titan Quest that is consistently praised is the dual-mastery system, which has subsequently been used and improved in Grim Dawn. You choose a mastery at level two, and you can optionally choose a second mastery at level eight (level ten in Grim Dawn). There's no restriction on the second mastery, so a character with Warfare as the first mastery and Defence as the second mastery has the same skill choices as one who chose Defence first and Warfare second.

Some of the masteries had obvious synergies, for example Warfare and Defence are great if you want a straightforward sword and shield warrior character, but there are loads of viable combinations, and a further level of complex permutations due to the variety of skills available in each mastery.

Generally, focussing on a small number of complementary skills and maxing them out tends to be better than putting a few points in a large number of skills, but some skills work well as 'one-pointers' for specific character builds. No build could be considered 'wrong' but some builds are much better than others, and some strong builds are not particularly fun to play.

With Titan Quest, Oblivion, and an escalating obsession with Guild Wars, 2006 was a full-on RPG year for me. I almost didn't find time to play Just Cause, Call of Juarez, or Dark Messiah of Might and Magic. Almost.

2007 was a different kind of year. A couple of months into

it, I knew I was going to be a father by late October so I had to plan my life and my gaming around this forthcoming seismic shift of responsibility. The Lord of the Rings Online ('Lotro' from this point on) was due to come out in April, and I was faced with a tough decision. Was I going to avoid it completely, or was I going to start playing it, knowing I'd have to quit later in the year and probably never go back to it? Ben, Carl, Silky and some other gamers from work were all planning to get it, and I didn't want to miss out. It sounded like it was going to be a WoW-clone, but set in the world of Middle Earth. I'd read the books, watched the films, played The Hobbit text adventure on a ZX Spectrum when our only weapons had been words, and I was excited about the whole 'running around being a Hobbit' game concept. It sounded silly enough that I had to play it.

A month before Lotro came out, we finally got a release of Stalker: Shadow of Chernobyl, a game Ben and I had been waiting ages to play. The finished game looked nothing like the pre-alpha demo we'd played a few years earlier; the game engine was totally different, and the gameplay was punishingly harsh. Stalker was okay, and I did play it a lot, but I think we'd hyped ourselves up over it to the point where it was never going to be as good as we had convinced ourselves it was going to be.

Bioshock came out in August, bad timing for me because I was only a couple of months away from fatherhood, and by that time I was spending as much time as possible in Lotro's version of Middle Earth. I didn't play Bioshock enough to get into it, and I have to accept it's one of many great games I either didn't play as much as I could have done, or never played at all.

Crysis and The Witcher came out late in 2007 but I didn't get around to playing either of them until 2008. Crysis felt like more of the same, coming from the people behind Far Cry, but it was still a lot of fun. The Witcher was great, a proper medieval fantasy badass game with some genuinely astonishing 'adult' content, from the cards collected after every amorous encounter to quests that dangled 'alternative rewards' in front of the player, such as a coven of vampires offering to bonk your brains out in exchange for not wantonly slaughtering them. I thought the final cinematic cut-scene after you'd completed the game was excellent.

Lotro came out on the twenty-fourth of April 2007, exactly six months before my son was born. I knew it was going to be about six months so I bought a six-month game pass for Lotro, created a Burglar Hobbit character called Muddy and ventured forth into the world. Ben's character was a Hunter Hobbit called Bones. I promised everyone, including myself, that I'd play Lotro properly, meaning I'd do all the quests and level up appropriately instead of spending my time jumping up and down on beds and wandering into high-level zones on suicidal sightseeing trips.

For the first few levels, I did what most people do: I figured out where the starter-area quests and auction house were, and I did all the 'collect 10 wolf pelts' type noob quests while I got familiar with the interface and the map and the quest log and the combat mechanics and the game chat and everything else.

Ben and I joined a guild called Jesters of Middle Earth because they sounded a lot less serious or power-levelly than some of the other guilds. I think Silky, and possibly also Carl, joined the far more noble sounding Guardians of Middle Earth, but we still occasionally met up with them if we were all logged on at the same time.

Although I'd promised to play the game properly, I'd picked the name Muddy for a reason, and it wasn't exactly sensible. Before I reached level fifteen, when it was finally possible to choose a surname for your character, the name Muddy seemed silly but fairly innocuous. Gaining a surname changed all that, because now there was a Hobbit called Muddy Nutsack in the game. The name made perfect sense on a puerile level: Hobbits are short, therefore their nutsacks would be muddy. I'd been worried right up until level fifteen that the censorship filter would prevent me using the word nutsack, but it didn't. A Hobbit called Muddy Pants would have been okay, but I had my heart set on Muddy Nutsack. The poet in me knew this was the name he deserved.

Chapter 13

History is our playground
'War, war never changes.'

Muddy Nutsack was a busy Hobbit. He took the profession 'Tinker', which meant he could cook, mine, and craft jewellery. At a high level of jewellery crafting, he could name the trinkets he crafted, and they were permanently labelled 'Made by Muddy'. If you're an MMO player, you're going to think that's pretty cool. If you're not an MMO player, you're going to think I'm a tragic loser. All I can say if you're in the latter group is: it's about time! The clues have been kind of obvious.

Muddy didn't bother much with cooking until late in the game, when a couple of friendly Hobbits provided a massive amount of raw fruit to assist with power-levelling Muddy's cookery skills. Those Hobbits were rewarded with overpowered pies of ultra-buffage and some magic necklaces and rings with stupid names. Tolkien would have been proud. Peter Jackson would have made a whole new three-film series and the pies alone would have had a twenty-million CGI budget.

The way any kind of crafting works in an MMO is, first

and most importantly, it's a massive grind and an infinite time-sink. Levelling the jewellery skill involved crafting thousands of rings and necklaces. To craft any item of jewellery, raw materials were needed. The most basic raw material was always some kind of metal. To get the metal, you needed to either buy it from the auction house - also known as throwing your money away - or you had to mine the ore yourself. Mining was a skill that had to be levelled up if you wanted to mine the more expensive metals, which you'd definitely need to be doing if you were levelling up your jewellery skill. Unsurprisingly, mining was a massive grind and an infinite time-sink.

To craft extremely high-level jewellery, in addition to needing the highest level metals, you needed to obtain the crafting recipes, usually unfeasibly rare loot drops, and you also needed some kind of special ingredient, almost always loot drops from an ultra-hard boss monster. Obtaining unfeasibly rare loot drops involved extreme farming. Obtaining loot drops from ultra-hard boss monsters involved camping a spawn location for ages, fighting the boss for twenty minutes, then getting killed just before a gold-farming bot walked up and took the loot.

Meanwhile, there was a whole MMO to play, and a lot of serious players to laugh at.

Rivendell in Lotro was a lovely place, they really did a great job of making it look right. That was the big difference between Lotro and WoW, Lotro's lore and locations were based on lore and locations we already knew and loved. A big city in WoW was a big city in WoW; it might look nice but it was just a location in a video game. The Shire was The freakin' Shire, man. Rivendell was goddamn Rivendell. To some extent, much of the positive impact of Lotro was the result of decades of conditioning. If you'd read the books and seen the films, going into the game felt like taking a journey into your own fantastic memories. Or maybe I'm talking a load of crap and we just enjoyed collecting boar stomachs, killing the same goblins over and over again, and grinding on thousands of maggots to get an achievement.

The Hobbit class 'Burglar' was a stealthy backstabber, much like a rogue or thief class in any other RPG. I've always liked stealth in video games, whether the whole game is based on the concept or it's a small component part of a bigger game. In Lotro, Muddy's sneaky skills gave me alternative ways of completing some quests. Where a character with a more frontal-assault set of skills would have to fight through an entire camp to reach a target boss, Muddy could sneak past everyone to the boss, backstab him and sneak away before anyone else noticed. Stealthily backstabbing everyone in the camp was also fun.

Some skills were only useful when you were in a team. Muddy had a skill that caused enemies to randomly attack each member of the team, presumably to counter enemy AI targeting the party healer. Ben and I figured out the skill was completely overpowered if there were only two of us in the team. Muddy would hit an enemy boss with the 'random attack' skill while Bones and Muddy were standing a long way from each other with the enemy boss between us. Bones would shoot it with a crippling arrow shot and it would slowly limp back and forth from one of us to the other while we took turns shooting and stabbing it until it was dead. We started calling it The Tennis Skill because of the effect it had on enemies.

Ben and I both failed to succumb to the 'ding/gratz' MMO mentality, so we were never real MMO players. Every time we saw some hardcore gaming legend announcing 'Ding!' in guild chat, we'd laugh at their 1337 skillz and go back to playing tennis with a nearby warg boss. I'm going to make an assumption here that not everyone will know about dinging. Some MMO players announce their level-up progress in game chat by typing 'Ding!' when they go up a level. There's some historical significance to this, where levelling up was accompanied by a 'ding' sound effect in an old role-playing game. 'Gratz' is the standard response, where random players congratulate a dinger on going from level 23 to 24, for example. Other, more honest responses would be 'Nobody cares' and 'Get a life'. When I maxed out Muddy at level fifty, I believe my in-game announcement was 'Now what?' which was either self-aware commentary, beta-meta, or just as pointless as saying 'ding'.

As planned, I quit playing Lotro when my son was born. I sold all my non-tradeable gear to an NPC shopkeeper and gave all my gold and tradeable gear to Ben. I logged out of the game and never went back. Hard stop. Cold turkey. Call it what you like, in the general scheme of things all I had done was stopped playing a video game. But I didn't completely stop playing video games, I just had a short break. Maybe a week.

2008 wasn't the absolute best year for PC game releases, but it had its fair share of decent ones. I had problems running GTAIV, mostly due to my PC not being able to run it at an acceptable speed, so I never played it very much. When it came out, I didn't have time to waste on games that didn't run well on my PC.

Some of the games that ran fine, and I managed to find the time to play, included Spore (which ended up being a waste of time), Fallout 3, Dead Space, Mirror's Edge, Race Driver Grid, Far Cry 2, Assassin's Creed, and Mass Effect. Spelunky was a freeware indie game that first appeared in 2008 and has since undergone significant updates and a full-on re-release. If you like platform games, you absolutely have to play it.

The demo of Spore was better than the full game. As anticlimactic disappointments go, Spore stole the crown. And the DRM on it was some kind of ridiculous bullshit that could have been a virus given the grief it caused me and countless other players.

Fallout 3 was great. It had nothing in common with Fallout and Fallout 2, apart from the post-apocalyptic theme and a fairly decent attempt to make a first-person shooting-based RPG with elements of a rehabilitated drunk's memories of Fallout clumsily shoehorned into it. I bought a special edition of the game which came with a metal model of a

Fallout dude wearing Brotherhood Outcast power armour. I gave it to Carl to paint it properly because the original paintjob was something shitty done by a machine. Carl is an amazing model painter, and he did a great job on my Fallout 3 model.

Fallout 3 was a victim of good intentions. The original Fallout games had choices and consequences, but these were generally subtle, or part of an extended plot twist or shocking end-of-game reveal. You could choose to do something that felt like a benevolent decision, and it might cause something bad to happen, or you might be forced into making a choice between two equally grim options. And then there was Fallout 3, where one of the first settlements you found had a live, unexploded nuclear bomb sitting in the middle of it. You could choose to detonate it, which was obviously a Bad Thing, but it was too tempting to ignore, not because we all wanted to be that dude from Dr Strangelove but because we wanted to see the big explosion. Yay, fireworks! What Fallout 3 did was trivialise atomic genocide for the sake of a pretty mushroom cloud cut-scene. I'm not complaining about the glorification of the mass vaporisation of a bunch of NPCs, I'm complaining that the choice wasn't driven by any kind of in-game morality or lack thereof, and you could always save the game before blowing the place up and then load the game and not blow it up.

Everyone remembers that bomb, but a far smaller number of Fallout 3 players remember the main quest, let alone completed it. As in Oblivion's open world, there was more fun to be had exploring the wasteland of Fallout 3 than plodding through the main quest. Fallout 3 also had a considerable amount of gore and dismemberment, and the Deathclaws were genuinely scary.

Talking of gore and dismemberment, Dead Space went above and beyond the nauseating visceral visual requirements of an homage to (not a rip-off of) Alien, The Thing and Event Horizon. The story was a copy/paste space sci-fi cliché: bad things have happened in space, you're on your own to investigate and ultimately sort it all out, meanwhile the aggressive alien mutant scum will get bigger and nastier the further you progress through the game. The over-the-shoulder viewpoint was a bit clunky, they might as well have had a message on the wall, finger-written in blood, that said 'Console port' next to the finger-written blood message that said 'Cut off their limbs'. As a survival-horror-in-space game, it was definitely a success, although some of the scripted encounters felt a bit too scripted, and there's a limit to the number of jump-scares you can have in dark, claustrophobic corridors before they lose the element of surprise.

Mass Effect was another game set in space, but it was a totally different experience compared to Dead Space, apart from the over-the-shoulder combat viewpoint because it was a console port. As Commander Shephard, you went on a journey through a universe of role-playing, action, dodgy moon buggies, failed conversations, abandoned crew members and bonking aliens. It was mostly a top-quality, triple-A game, with a few exceptions that weren't significant enough to totally screw up the experience.

Games like Fallout 3, Mass Effect, and Titan Quest (and its excellent expansion pack) stuck around on my hard drive for a long time, so I was spending more time on those games in 2009 than on games released that year. 2009's Dragon Age Origins was one minor exception, a party-based RPG that was fun for a while but ultimately got left behind after I lost interest. I put a scruffy but comical video on YouTube, featuring partially naked Dragon Age Origins characters running around with the Benny Hill theme playing in the background. It's still there, on the Arcadelife YouTube channel, if you want to waste a few minutes of your life watching a blocky dwarf character jogging around in his pants, being chased by the rest of the party.

The only other 2009 game I played with any degree of enthusiasm was The Saboteur, and I actually completed that one. It didn't sound like it was going to be great, a mashup of Assassin's Creed's pseudo-parkour environmental exploration, Mafia-style driving-and-crime missions, and a World War 2 setting with a protagonist who was a sex-case discount Indiana Jones with a tendency to attach remote detonated explosives to cows. For all its blatant plagiarism and wanton lack of originality, The Saboteur managed to lump all the borrowed ideas and gameplay features together in a consistently entertaining way.

From my perspective, 2009 was another of those anticlimactic years for PC game releases; in contrast, 2010 was a far more memorable year. The majority of my 2010 gaming time was spent on Just Cause 2, Alan Wake, Mafia 2, Fallout New Vegas, and Limbo.

The demo for Just Cause 2 was a crazy amount of fun. It had a session time limit, but almost immediately there was an unofficial patch available online to disable it so you could play the demo for as long as you liked. The fun in Just Cause 2 came from the combination of crazy toys (grappler, parachute, explosives), loads of different vehicles, massive explosions, and a gorgeous open-world environment where most things could be flown, driven, climbed or blown up.

For someone who goes into most games looking for the highest building or mountain to jump off, or to try to build a tower of military vehicles and then blow it up in the style of a psychotic Fred Dibnah, the Just Cause 2 demo was pure gold. I started off being moderately restrained, just attaching gas cylinders to NPCs and launching them into the sky, but it wasn't long before I was grappling barrels to planes and doing airborne impersonations of the shark from Jaws after they attached all those barrels to it.

As open-world playgrounds go, JC2 was the best I'd seen. The demo was endlessly replayable, and the full game almost lived up to the expectations it set. Playing the demo over and over again was a choice; completing base takeover missions again and again in the full game eventually became tedious and annoying. Some of the main missions were frustrating enough to deter progress, the real fun of the game was always its ridiculous physics and the temptation to try something stupid just 'cause you could. Surfing on a huge transport plane was fun, and in JC2 you could do that, then jump off and blow the plane up with a rocket launcher before aerial hijacking the military chopper sent to apprehend you. I burned up countless hours driving around the JC2 map looking for stupidly placed ramps, or roads that led high up into the mountains. It was the best game ever, until I inevitably got tired of it.

I played Mafia 2 all the way through to its grim, downbeat ending. In many ways it was the perfect video game sequel, ditching the bits that spoiled the first one and tightening everything else up, with an absolutely cracking main story and a gritty, realistic world to explore.

Limbo is a cult classic, and like a lot of games, films, books and music in that category, it's not going to appeal to everyone. Particularly if you're at all squeamish and you don't like spiders. At times, Limbo felt like a nightmarish death simulator rather than a platform game. You die a lot, and most deaths are horrifyingly brutal, and it's worse because it happens to this cute, innocent, childlike main character. I mistyped that as 'maim character' and almost left it in.

Fallout New Vegas, sorry I never finished you. I tried, I really did. I even dabbled with your hardcore mode but it turned a grim wasteland RPG into a frustrating radiation-sickness and starvation simulator. The guns were cool, but I suspect by the time I wandered out into the wasteland for the fiftieth time, I was already turning into a gaming lightweight.

I'd like to blame Ben for my descent into the comfortable hell of casual games, but I can honestly only blame myself.

Ben just encouraged me, a lot. We were playing Angry Birds when it first came out, when it was a fairly original physics puzzle game, long before it turned into yet another soulless money-grubbing franchise in the vanguard of the pay-to-play world-domination invasion.

Angry Birds and Doodle Jump; there was a time when those were two of the must-have phone games, when they were the only popular phone games and we thought they were great. There was even a time when Gameloft made decent pay-once games, as hard as that is to comprehend, let alone believe. Dungeon Hunter was a nice game. The first one, not any of the sequels, each one of those moving Gameloft a step closer to the abyss of in-app purchases and shameful pay-to-win crap. They had a God of War clone called Hero of Sparta which was pretty good, albeit massively derivative. It was part of a game giveaway special event where Gameloft made a load of their games free for a few hours each, and I remember I wanted to get Hero of Sparta for free so badly I got totally obsessed with their giveaway and I even started following Gameloft on Twitter to get the announcements. Tragic times. Ben couldn't believe I was so obsessed with it, but I got the game for free and I definitely had my money's worth out of it.

"If you want free games, you should do a review website," Ben told me, and it was kind of a joke, and also kind of not a joke. I enjoyed writing game reviews, and I'd written quite a few for his PDA website so he knew it was the kind of thing I'd be able to do. It had never occurred to me that I should write reviews for a site of my own, and start asking game companies for promo codes to get free games. We talked about it off and on for a while through 2010, but I didn't do anything about it until the first month of 2011.

Chapter 14
Arcadelife
'It's the best game ever this week.'

Mobile touch-screen games weren't all cuddly, casual and cute, some of them were proper games.

Galaxy on Fire 2 was a full-featured space game with everything you'd expect: spaceships, space battles, trading, exploration, mining asteroids for resources, hiring wingmen, researching ship upgrades, saving up loads of space cash to buy the best ship in the game, all of that and more.

Infinity Blade started out as a flashy tech demo using the Unreal engine; the game itself was a surprisingly addictive fantasy beat-em-up with a huge amount of unlockable weapons and armour, and a swipe-based control method that was not only playable and fun but nothing like the frustrating disaster we all expected it to be. It was a repetitive game, but instead of pretending it wasn't, they built the gameplay and the progression system around the fact that everything was repeated over and over. I played Galaxy on Fire 2 and Infinity Blade a lot, probably more than I played some of the less-interesting PC games over the years.

Before Gameloft went full in-app-purchase (IAP) greed, their last half-decent game was Order and Chaos Online, a cheap WoW clone for mobile devices that turned out to be a heck of a lot better than it sounds. I was in there from the start, so I not only witnessed the game's decline into cynical pay-to-win lameness first-hand but I was also able to create a character called Order and another one called Chaos. I joined a guild owned by a player called Undead, obviously another early adopter, and I played through all the original content with the Chaos character, a bog-standard warrior, using two-handed melee weapons. Much later, when most of the original players in Undead's guild had given up, I swapped to the Order character, a healer, and rushed through most of the content again in a two-player team with a bloke called Trevor who was levelling a similar warrior character to Chaos. Soloing the game was a decent way to pass the time, but regularly teaming up with Trevor in a clichéd but powerful warrior-plus-healer combo meant we were able to burn through the game extremely quickly.

Although the basic elements of a WoW clone were mostly present and correct, Order and Chaos Online had no endgame at all. There weren't even any main quests after you reached level fifty-seven, and the cap was sixty, so if you wanted to reach max level the only option was to grind all the high-level daily quests until you maxed out. And then there was literally nothing left to do, apart from duel with other players or lurk in low-level mandatory PVP zones to annoy other players. I never did that PVP annoying thing, but I met other pointless muppets who were doing it while I was levelling up.

There were still a few players left in Undead's guild when the first set of pay-to-win armour appeared in the in-game store. A couple of guild members bought it and wore it, but those of us who hadn't thrown money at Gameloft's cash-grab nonsense were glad to set them right in guild chat, telling them they were wearing The Gear of Shame. But it was the beginning of the end for Order and Chaos - the game and my two characters - the point where all pretence at providing a cheap WoW clone was abandoned, casually sacrificed on the satanic altar of in-app-purchases.

The first iOS game reviews were posted on the Arcadelife website in February 2011. In that month, I reviewed twenty-seven games and posted a couple of articles related to gaming in general but focussing on popular iOS games at the time. The reviews included Tiny Wings - the first 'Tiny Wings' type game, unsurprisingly - Hunters Episode One, a turn-based action game with an Aliens feel to it, and Battleheart, which was an excellent game, so good that I posted two reviews of it: one written by me and one written by Ben. It was the only time I ever posted a review written by someone else. The very first review was posted on the first of February, and it was for an endless runner game called Grim Joggers.

One of the articles I wrote in February 2011 has the title 'Naming stuff in games is fun'. I was obviously not a big fan of subtlety or tabloid newspaper headline puns when it came to the Arcadelife article titles. The article focuses mostly on

Game Dev Story, a tycoon style game where you take control of a game development company. The game itself is hellishly addictive, and you get plenty of opportunities to call your games outlandish names. From the article, screenshots show some of the games I invented were called 'Angry Noobs', 'Napalm Grandad', 'Eunuch Ninja', and 'God vs Batman'.

Ben and I found the word 'polished' amusing, as it tended to be used in almost every iOS game review ever written. I contributed to the spread of the outbreak by using it on a frequent basis in Arcadelife reviews.

Arcadelife worked out much better than I'd expected, as both a review site and a method of legitimately obtaining free copies of new iOS games. I only requested promo codes for games where I was reasonably confident the game, and my review of it, would be good. This didn't stop people sending me unsolicited promo codes, and I always tried to review any game I was given. There were exceptions, but if a game was so bad, or so unlike the kind of game I could realistically enjoy, I'd send an email to them, explaining the reasons why I wouldn't be reviewing the game on Arcadelife.

I received a lot of positive feedback for my reviews, frequently from the smaller indie developers who hadn't managed to get any other sites to review their games. The Arcadelife reviews were short, but I always tried to make them entertaining. For a long time, I used song lyrics as a tag-line for each review, with every lyric linked to the source album on iTunes, or a YouTube video on the rare occasions the song wasn't on iTunes.

I added to the volume of reviews by reviewing some of the games I bought, and I applied the logic that if I'd paid for the game I could say whatever I wanted about it, even if it wasn't exactly kind, providing it was a true and accurate opinion, not just taking the piss out of a game for the sake of it.

I only ever took one review down after posting it, because the developer contacted me and started asking for detailed technical reasons why I hadn't given the game a good review. After a couple of back-and-forth emails, I decided it was going to be a lot easier to delete the review than to leave it there, where it wasn't doing anyone any good, and where it was also causing me loads more grief than necessary.

Generally, the vast majority of developers and publishers who contacted me did so to tell me how much they liked a review of their game. The German developers of a vampire-themed endless runner changed the name of the game to one I suggested, after I told them their original name wasn't as good as it could be. One of the developers put me in touch with a freelance artist a couple of years later, and I commissioned his work for the covers of my two vampire novels.

Another iOS game developer added a high-score achievement into his game after I figured out a way to get crazy scores by doing something he'd never considered; the achievement was called The Arcadelife Cup. Sadly, the game is no longer available on the App store, like a lot of games that never got updated to 64-bit compatibility when iOS 11 came out.

The first interview posted on Arcadelife was with Quantum Sheep, the developer of several very cool iOS games. He had a similar gaming life history to me, with a few highlights of extreme gaming geek-out that almost put mine in the shade. For example, I've never had a Tetris birthday cake.

I also interviewed Keith Otto from Ramble Interactive, the developer of Toxic Frog and Revenge of Toxic Frog. Revenge was the game with the Arcadelife Cup achievement, one of my favourite indie arcade games for iOS devices. At the time of the interview, Ramble Interactive was based in Escondido, near San Diego, so the interview was done via email. Actually, all the Arcadelife interviews were done that way because I 'embrace modern technological solutions going forwards in the communications space'. See how utterly ridiculous that sounds? Office-speak, also known as the death of everything.

The most famous person I interviewed for Arcadelife was Jeff Minter, at a time when he was creating some truly wonderful games for iOS devices. I was pleased with the way the interview turned out, although it was weird trying to be a proper journo when all I was really doing at the time was posting fairly silly reviews of phone games on a blog. The first question in the interview with Jeff was 'How big is your farm?', and it just got better and better after that.

When I started writing this book, I promised myself I wouldn't just 'do a Brooker' and compile a book from a pile of my old reviews, no matter how entertaining Charlie's books turned out to be. If he ever reads this (yeah, I know he won't) I'd just like to point out that I have read most of his books, I enjoyed them, and I'm not imitating his work in any way in this book.

However, I did change my mind about not padding this chapter out with some of my favourite excerpts from the Arcadelife website reviews, so that's what you've got coming up for the next few pages. The reviews are for iOS games from 2011-2012, and the majority of the games are no longer available which, in a small number of cases, is a real shame.

During 2011, I was coming to the end of a long period of employment due to taking 'voluntary' redundancy because my job was about to be outsourced to a couple of companies in India, which left me unemployed for the whole of 2012. The following review text is lifted from the reviews I wrote back then, so some of the anger, bitterness, self-mockery, and total lack of self-respect of those times shows up quite frequently in these snippets. Have fun, here we go…

Game: Carmageddon. Review date 19 October 2012

Ban this sick filth! Sorry, my mistake – that was 1997. I have fond memories of Carmageddon (1997 – PC), specifically the patched 'Splat Pack' version where all the blood, guts and other banned content had been reinstated following the nanny state do-gooder censorship of the initial release. I was concerned that the iOS release would fall far short of my admittedly rose-tinted (gore-tinted more like) memories, and I was very surprised and impressed when it didn't.

Game: Angry Baba. Review date 13 October 2012

Ridiculous, inexplicable and repetitive. One of the funniest games ever. I can't begin to explain how daft, yet utterly enjoyable this game is. The app store description alone is worth the price of admission and the game exceeds even the wildest expectations you might have after reading that.

The bad news: Nobody will play it and the world will be a sadder place because of this.

Picture the scene: My four-year-old son has just cleared the first few levels of Polyroll (good for him, at least he's leading a productive life, right?) and he gets a bit bored of that – no criticism of Polyroll, he gets bored of everything very quickly – so he starts looking at the icons on my iPad and decides he wants to play Angry Baba. Don't ask me why – the icon is as bizarre as the rest of the game. So anyway, after I explain how to play – like I have the slightest idea – he has a few goes and declares it to be the best game ever. I'm not one to argue with a four-year-old's judgement, particularly when it involves video games, so I start getting into the game and discover, much to my surprise and not a small amount of horror, that he is right. It is indeed the best game ever. It's silly, incomprehensible, completely bonkers, and none of that really matters. Any game that prompts the questions "why are those mammoths helping us?" and "do all cavemen punch flying rocks?" is an essential purchase as far as I'm concerned.

Game: The Lords of Midnight. Review date 22 December 2012

If you love a game, love the game's creator, and want to produce an updated tribute – here's your benchmark. Almost thirty years old and yet it feels fresh, relevant and completely at home on a touch screen. Recommended without reservation – so good it makes me want to cry.

Game: Meganoid 2. Review date 26 November 2012

Evoking memories of Rick Dangerous, Meganoid 2 has gone for a more focussed theme than its predecessor and I feel this works in its favour. If you are unfamiliar with Rick Dangerous, just think of Indiana Jones taking on a series of death-defying challenges devised by a very angry Yoda and you'll be somewhere close to what this game is all about.

Game: Bad Piggies. Review date 4 October 2012

Due to the fundamental stupidity of human beings, Rovio were never going to avoid a barrage of frothing temper tantrums on the app store when they released a game that wasn't yet another Angry Birds sequel. However, if your age is in double figures and you have posted a one-star review for Bad Piggies along the lines of "WTF borrrring can't play it bring back angry birds" then you seriously need to get a bloody life.

So where does that leave us, apart from wanting to live on the moon and get away from all the freakin' idiots on this planet? Bad Piggies is pretty good. It's not a stunning, jaw-dropping phenomenon, but maybe that's not altogether a bad thing. Cobbling together a rickety cart from a few wooden crates and an electric fan, then watching it fail to climb a gentle slope is a curiously amusing way to pass the time, and a decent alternative to shooting zombies, racing cars, jumping around on platforms and, of course I have to say it, flinging flightless birds at pigs in wooden forts.

Game: Wild Blood. Review date 6 September 2012

Big swords, pretty graphics, multiplayer. What's to dislike? Let's see… Sorry, but I can't help it; a much-hyped Gameloft game turns up and it's impossible to resist taking a few cheap shots at it. Originality, what's that? Oh, come on, it's flippin' Gameloft. Anyone expecting this to be original hasn't been paying attention for the last few years. Gameloft don't do 'original'.

Oh dear, I'm having so much fun with this game that it almost makes me feel guilty. "That's a Gameloft game, you can't be enjoying that!" etc. But I am, and quite a lot. The story is completely daft, which is nice.

Game: Gibbets 2. Review date 15 September 2012

Shoot the ropes, save the dangling Coldplay fans.

Game: Happy Street. Review date 2 August 2012

'Happy Street'? It's more like 'IAP-y Street'. Looks pretty, though. Once you start thinking you might be enjoying the game, progress starts to slow right down unless you're happy (ha ha, happy!) throwing real money at it. Apart from that, which should ruin it for anyone who isn't completely stupid, it crashes a lot.

Game: Flying Kritters. Review date 29 August 2012

It's boring, badly derivative, slow, occasionally jerky, has adverts at the start, Game Center failure messages, and when you scroll through the character list it eventually locks up and you have to close it down and restart it. Music is a repetitive, forgettable tune; sounds are limited to plinky-plinky noises when you collect coins. There are vertical lines where some of the landscape graphics join up; don't ask me what the technical term for that is, probably something like "couldn't be bothered to get it right".

People need to try harder. If you're going to blatantly copy a good game, at least try to make your version at least half as good as the one you're imitating.

Game: Lego App 4+. Review date 16 July 2012

I love the app store, I really do. Where else can you see dozens of otherwise completely anonymous and pointless people lining up to show the world how stupid they are? To all the elite gamers posting one-star reviews of this game with comments such as "Boring I completed it in a few seconds" – congratulations, you are not a four-year-old child. Well done, now don't forget to let the door labelled "Morons This Way" hit you in the ass on your way out.

Game: Manos - The Hand of Fate. Review date 29 July 2012

Graphically, it is an 8-bit memory reborn on your i-device. The sounds are wonderfully prehistoric too. What is most impressive is the convincingly ultra-retro gameplay. You run, you jump, you shoot, miss and die. Over and over again. I don't want to spoil it for you, but the big, nasty boss at the end of stage 3 is completely overshadowed by the screen-smashing frustration of stage 4. That's as far as I've got so far, but I keep going back because I remember this kind of eternal struggle from the dawn of ZX Spectrum gaming and I will not give up. Not today anyway.

Game: Astronot. Review date 25 June 2012

Quite fantastic, really. I know I sound like I'm doing an Emperor's New Clothes review here, pointing at something with two frames of animation and the colour palette of Clive Sinclair's underpants and going, "Ooh, it's brilliant because it's retro," but it is. If you wanted a definitive example of "gameplay over graphics", Astronot would be it.

Game: Battlefield Minesweeper. Review date 11 May 2011

A few years ago I wrote an Asteroids clone for the PC using GameMaker. Apart from the graphics, which are hard to perfectly recreate using sprites, the game played about as close to the original as I believe it was possible for me to achieve. I added a second mode, where a timer constantly ran out unless you shot something, and you only had one life. I did this for my own amusement and I would never consider trying to foist it onto an indifferent world because, as I would be the first to admit, the world doesn't need another version of Asteroids. I guess that's this review done.

Game: Gaga Duck. Review date 2 May 2012

I'll keep on reviewing these games that nobody else seems to review, or notice, or care about, because sometimes I blunder across a real gem. This, however, is not one of those days.

Game: Spellsword. Review date 28 April 2012

Life sucks and video games are trivial time-wasters at best. I could be doing so much more with my time than reviewing spare-change phone games, but I'm not. Maybe one day I'll look back at all this and ask myself why, but I seriously doubt it. Overall, this game is a lot of fun and you should get it.

Game: Prince of Persia Classic. Review date 26 April 2012

Stupid IAPs. Seriously, if you're willing to spend $99.99 on extra lives for a fairly weak iPad game, I think you have some problems. The graphics, although nice, are not quite as mind-blowing as Ubisoft would like you to think they are. Animation looks less fluid than in the original 1989 game… just think about that for a few seconds. Controls are annoying and unreliable, deaths feel cheap and unfair on a regular basis.

Game: Shark Dash. Review date 20 April 2012

Ok, it's a good game, I admit it. Now can we move on, forget this ever happened and look forward to the next bloated, Freemium IAP-abusing joke so that we all know normal Gameloft service has been resumed? This game doesn't even feel like a Gameloft game, and these days that is a definite plus point.

Game: Box Cat. Review date 29 March 2012

Wrap your head around this concept: You guide a large square cat back and forth, left and right, across a busy road, smacking cars into one another and causing combo car crashes. There's no reason for any of this and it remains bafflingly ridiculous, the craziness escalating exponentially with every weird new cat character that you unlock. In my view, this is an essential game.

Game: Coco Loco. Review date 28 March 2012

Ultimately, if you take a one-trick pony and give him a pink neon saddle and flashing hooves, most people will still see that he's the same old one-trick pony.

Game: Swordigo. Review date 22 March 2012

Stunning, flawless and way too much fun. If you have a friend with an iOS device, and they don't know about this game, go and tell them about it. Or send them a text, or an email, whatever. Tell them to buy it; hell, tell them I told them to buy it. It doesn't matter. They need this game and so do you.

Game: Islands of Diamonds. Review date 12 March 2012

It could be great, but the controls (and by that I mean the lack of control) plus some truly challenging (and by that I mean stupidly difficult) tracks make any progress beyond the second island an exercise in the kind of tooth-grinding persistence that only a tiny minority will be willing to endure. If you thought that sentence was rather awkward, there's no way you're ready for Islands of Diamonds.

Game: Neoteria. Review date 10 March 2012

The app store description includes a warning that this "is not for the weak or casual gamer". If the intention is to alienate a large number of potential players and reduce the money that this game makes, that's really great. Otherwise, maybe try catering for the "weak or casual gamer" by adding a mode with auto-fire and removing some of the enemies that take a lot more than one hit to destroy. I wouldn't describe myself as a casual gamer but the novelty of pounding the hell out of an on-screen fire button (and fighting the annoyance of directional controls that frequently let me down) dwindled pretty damn fast for me.

The combination of infinite lives and a power-up penalty doesn't work. It spoils the game. It isn't fun. Nobody wants to grind for power-ups just to die due to unreliable controls and lose the damn power-ups, and yet that seems to me to be the only viable way to play the game. It isn't even satisfying. There's too much wrong with this, I'm afraid, for me to pull out the nostalgia card and tell anyone it's a great game. I'll look forward to the update that fixes the controls and adds some retro fun to the retro graphics.

Closing thought: R-Type completely nailed this genre a long, long time ago. If you're going to reinvent the wheel, at least make the damn thing round.

Game: Midway Arcade. Review date 28 February 2012

Spy Hunter is all you need to play in order to understand what I was saying: our memories of classic arcade games are often seriously let down by the reality of playing them again now. Jaw-droppingly primitive and crippled by woefully inadequate touch controls, it's like being groped by your drunk grandad who you never really fancied that much anyway.

Game: Gridrunner. Review date 24 February 2012

Gridrunner for iOS is an 80's arcade game the way we'd like to remember them, not the way they really were. That's a good thing, and also a rather fantastic achievement. Jeff has held back on the psychedelia and minotaurs this time and the game is better for it. Not that I have anything against those traditional Llamasoft game elements, but Gridrunner – pure arcade classic reinvention on a touch-screen device – doesn't need any of that in order to succeed quite spectacularly at what it's trying to do.

Game: Fishbowl Racer. Review date 20 Fenruary 2012

Excellent game. Once you start getting into the 'shelf combos' it's just a whole new level of genius. I don't know who they've got working at Donut Games, designing this stuff, but they're bloody good at it.

Game: Necrorun. Review date 5 February 2012

I could play this all night. The unlockable powers not only add great replay incentive but also prove to be invaluable as soon as you try stage 2 and the ****ing archers start appearing! If you like endless runners, particularly ones with a bit of depth in the upgrade department and a rather cool theme – you play as Death on a horse, killing everything including trees – go get this right now.

Game: Robokill 2. Review date 4 February 2012

The IAPs are baffling – you can buy your way to level 17 without shooting a single alien. Well that's just great; why not let us buy the congratulatory "Thanks for saving the universe" final cutscene or, better still, why not just go and watch someone else playing the game on YouTube? Pathetic. I honestly don't care what the mathematically calculated final rating is for this, it's getting a low mark for the total lack of inspiration and the sheep-like "must add IAPs" attitude.

Game: Rabit Maze (sic). Review date 4 January 2012

It exists and I have been exposed to it. That's 3 minutes of my life I'll never get back. Graphics – awful. No animation on sprites. Control method – dire. I probably shouldn't let it get to me, but this is just appallingly bad. It isn't worth the effort of providing constructive critical suggestions, as the whole point of this app appears to be to annoy people, particularly anyone gullible enough to buy it.

Game: Pixel Ball. Review date 30 December 2011

Minimalist visuals, uninspiring gameplay and poor paddle control. Well done.

Game: The Bard's Tale. Review date 13 December 2011

It's surprising how far games have advanced since 2004. I don't mean graphically, but there are lots of RPGs already available on the iOS devices that are a heck of a lot more fun than this. On an iPad it is just plain ugly. We can hold parties in the street for as long as we like, applauding the arrival of a massive (1.34gb download) "classic" role-playing game on the iOS platform, but ultimately it's not *the best game ever* and it never was.

Game: Dizzy - Prince of the Yolkfolk. Review date 12 December 2011

It should have been good, but it's not. Once they provide proper controls as an option, instead of the sanity-defying mess of randomly scattered buttons, and tune up the responsiveness and Dizzy's walking speed, then it's going to be slightly better than a dated, mediocre game. Until then, I can't recommend it. Dizzy fans in particular need to stay away, as the game creates that bizarre emotional mix where you're willing yourself to enjoy a game while simultaneously despising the people who have wrecked your rose-tinted memories by releasing such a poorly considered port.

Game: Snoopy's Street Fair. Review date 18 November 2011

I like the game, and I'll play it until I hit the IAP wall, then I'll give up. I'm not saying people are stupid spending real money just to keep playing this kind of Freemium title, just that I'd feel stupid if I ever considered doing it.

Game: Kick The Buddy. Review date 14 November 2011

Initially, I just thought "What is the point of this?" Then I saw something I wanted to unlock for $300 and kept smacking the poor little bastard around until I could afford it. Then I started wishing it had blood and gore, at which point I had to question my own sanity. So go ahead, get it, turn yourself into a desensitised monster, just like me.

Game: Sailor Dog. Review date 9 November 2011

I'm always dubious when another endless style game pops up for review, because I keep telling myself that there's really only so much that can be done with the genre. And, yet again, I'm proved wrong and I have to rethink my place in the cosmos and ask several deep and probing philosophical questions. Such as, "Why would a dog go sailing in an origami swan?" The answer is as easy as it is obvious – "Because it's a ****ing videogame, you gonk". And it's a damn good one at that.

Game: Lost Monsters. Review date 21 October 2011

The world is pretty much split into three camps: people who love match-3 games, people who don't, and people who have never played a videogame in their life. My main challenge right now is choosing something to review on a Saturday night when I'm tired, not sure whether I'm still hungry or not, and an as yet still-not-unwrapped iCade is sitting in a box on the floor of the room where I'm typing these very words.

Not a game: Animoog. Review date 20 October 2011

Yeah, ok, I know it's not a game. But it's fun and it's the same price (currently) as the cheapest non-free games on the app store. I blew 69p on it in a spontaneous impulse-buy, prompted by the nice screenshots. I can play the easy bits from the theme to Escape from New York and it sounds great on the Animoog, despite the fact that my musical ability peaked around 2002 while playing bass in a punk band, so I'm hardly qualified to talk about music. It's amusing to read reviews of the Animoog on proper music sites, where they bang on for the first ten paragraphs about historical and factual inaccuracies in the Animoog's app store description. See, I thought music was about having fun, but really it's about being a po-faced pedant who would bore an accountant to death. Get the app, get wasted and make some weird noises.

Game: Flick Soccer. Review date 16 October 2011

It's a good game, and so much more fun than listening to workmate 'A' cheerfully taking the piss out of workmate 'B' on a Monday morning because the team that workmate 'A' supports (called "We") won a game, and the team that workmate 'B' supports (called "You") didn't. Tragic. We all know that obsessively playing videogames is so much more manly.

Game: Scribblenauts Remix. Review date 13 October 2011

A lot of the entertainment on offer here depends on your vocabulary, imagination and how silly you want to be. Completing the beach party puzzle sensibly isn't as much fun as trying to kill everyone with sharks. Personally, I like watching pink robotic dinosaurs fight giant bald gorillas and I am endlessly fascinated by seeing what I can balance on top of a helicopter.

Game: Baby Bubblez. Review date 10 October 2011

This is pretty much what videogames should be all about – doing something fundamentally inexplicable as skilfully as possible.

Game: Where's My Water? Review date 24 September 2011

Finally I get to play a liquid-based physics game that doesn't involve teeth-grinding rage trying to place fiddly, illogical objects or attempting to collect randomly splattering and unconvincing glop in precariously balanced containers. Based on my experiences in the first twenty levels of Where's My Water?, none of the factors that ultimately reduce these games to a spiralling vortex of hatred (for me) appear to be present in this game. Witness my slack-jawed amazement that someone (Disney, for F's sake!) has managed to get a water-based physics puzzler so right.

Game: iSquares. Review date 21 September 2011

It's all a bit formal, like an office memo notifying you of some dismal nobody's appointment as your new manager.

Game: Lap Uranus. Review date 18 September 2011

Pun-splattered suicide mission blends puerile innuendo with intense gameplay. Looking beyond the arse jokes, it is actually a pretty good variation on the "endless travel" theme, although you're only ever travelling in circles. Around Uranus. If you find Benny Hill offensive, or you don't appreciate playground Uranus-pun humour, you will probably already be writing a frothing letter of complaint to Apple. If you fancy piloting a rocket around Uranus, with the huge possibility of ramming right into Uranus at high velocity, and you can't stop smirking at the idea of doing this, there's really nothing stopping you getting this game.

Game: Goat Up. Review date 17 September 2011

I couldn't get my feeble brain to adapt to Llamasoft's previous release (Deflex) but this one, for me, is just brilliant. Leaping around as a procreation-obsessed goat in a world of 80s gaming sprites and trippy weirdness is just pure fun. It makes me happy. Not many games do that nowadays and I don't think many developers put "Make the player happy" at the top of their list when designing a game.

Game: Babes vs Robots. Review date 13 September 2011

As with many iOS titles, a game that would struggle to get

beyond the initial-idea stage on any other platform appears quite normal and unsurprising as an iPhone release. The title "Babes vs Robots" is just as likely to repel as it is to attract, depending on your personal preferences, and the blatantly derivative combat style is also treading a thin line between "Instabuy" and "Oh no, not again". Dispensing with any attempt at common sense, I'd recommend forcefully violating your iTunes credit one more time in order to help these scantily clad saviours defend our planet from the Robot menace.

Game: Tapsteroids. Review date 4 September 2011

Not bad at all. Seriously, it's pretty good. You can tell I'm tired, can't you. Well, I'm sorry. I completely missed yesterday (no review or anything) because I was off having fun at the beach. I've just got home, unpacked, and I'm trying to write a quick review. Be thankful the game is decent or it would just be a load of swearing.

Game: Jetpack Joyride. Review date 2 September 2011

It's great to see a popular developer of casual phone games taking a stance against scientific research. If more developers, for example Rovio and whoever it was that made Doodlejump, got behind some serious campaigns like saving the ozone and shit, the world would be a better place. Look to Halfbrick and what they are achieving here with their outright condemnation of science, step up and follow their shining example. Right now, if a bunch of you went and got hold of some jetpacks and started collecting coins from secret research establishments it would be a great start. What are you waiting for?

Behind the commendable anti-science message is a game that is as addictive as a crack pipe dipped in chocolate.

Game: Fatcat Rush. Review date 1 September 2011

The cat character could do with looking a bit more like a cat. Bulba the Cat had the whole obese feline look spot-on. This one is a bit too square and not really looking much like a cat. Also, developers need to drop the "apathy achievements" where you get one for displaying the credits or looking at the help screen. It may have been ironically amusing the first time, but it's starting to become some kind of standard for iOS games now, which is rather uninspiring. Just stop it, please.

Game: Dust Those Bunnies. Review date 30 August 2011

Incredibly simplistic "slowly brush dust-bunnies into dustpan" gameplay sounds like the winning entrant in a contest to create the least exciting game concept ever. In practice it isn't vastly different from what you'd expect after reading the description. If you're considering creating a videogame, try asking a few random people what they think of your idea before spending months of your life turning it into a product that you intend to market to a potential global audience. Just a suggestion.

Game: Avadon - The Black Fortress. Review date 27 August 2011

Wildly generalising here, but I'd speculate that the average casual Angry Birds player would choke on their caramel macchiato just looking at the instructions menu for this game.

Game: Word Ball. Review date 21 August 2011

Anything with an online leaderboard invites cheating from those who feel insecure enough to need that kind of ego-bolstering. All you need is the pause button and a free online anagram solver and you too can be the best player in the world. Just don't.

Game: Let's Golf 3. Review date 13 August 2011

Beautiful, bloated, often laggy and unresponsive. Ruined by pay-to-play. You have 5 goes and then either wait for hours or dip into your iTunes credit. I know, you couldn't make this stuff up. The frequent lag, particularly the spikes when you're trying to set power or accuracy during a shot, are quite irritating. The complete downer, the reason this game should fail spectacularly, is the incredibly stupid continual "pay-to-play" money-making scheme, whereby you have energy points that are used up whenever you play or retry a hole.

Game: Emberwind. Review date 10 August 2011

They wouldn't let me use this in my iTunes review, but this is my site so I can say what I like: Fucking Brilliant. There you go.

Game: Connectrode. Review date 1 August 2011

This isn't the review just yet, this is me remembering the review in 2020... I remember this one because after I posted the review I received an email from someone linked to the game developers, explaining to me at length that I didn't appreciate the gameplay because I didn't understand it, that I was, in fact, an ignorant moron who wasn't clever enough to enjoy their excellent game.

This is most of the review:

It's like Tetris but without the gravity, kinetics and gameplay. You will like this game if you enjoy turn-based puzzle games where your opponent is the lack of an undo button. Somewhere between the initial concept and the finished product, the elements that make a game fun and challenging appear to have been lost along the way. It must have sounded like a good idea when it was initially being developed, but the end result is frankly quite boring – a bland and unimaginative version of match-3.

Looking back, I think I was a bit too generous. The game was fucking dire.

Game: Deflex. Review date 28 July 2011

I am in a tiny minority that just can't get on with this game. Listen to the universal acclaim and read the glowing reviews on the app store. If you're unlucky, like me, and your brain just refuses to comply with this game, just accept the fact and spend a few hours crying in a dark room. To avoid karmic repercussions, I shall award this game infinity out of infinity, because that's probably how long it would take me to get anywhere near mastering it.

Game: .Matrixx. Review date 18 July 2011

Some people won't understand why there's no tilt control and will start up their own pointless little political party just so they can campaign in the next general election to get tilt controls added to this game. Don't vote for them, people, they know not of what they blabber.

Game: Cuddle Bears. Review date 10 July 2011

Ok, I get how the name is ironic but did nobody think this through? An app store search for "cuddle bears" brings this up along with a bunch of cute, pointless apps for the under threes. If I hadn't been given this game to review, I would never, ever have looked at it. Because of the name. Can I make it any clearer? Good game let down by very, very ill-advised name choice. The characters are weird, yet consistent; the challenge is pretty much spot on; graphics are good, frame-rate is good, combos and achievements add that essential "one more go" factor. Hard to fault. Apart from, you know, the stupid ****ing name.

Game: Hard Lines. Review date 7 July 2011

If anything, this burned my battery out faster than The Dungeon Saga. Maybe that's because I played it non-stop for 3 days. Don't do that, kids, it's not a good idea.

Game: Backstab (Gameloft's Assassin's Creed 'homage'). Review date 4 July 2011

If you go in expecting it to be a fairly blatant Assassin's Creed rip-off but with a rather loose feeling and combat that is less about stealth kills and more of a button mashing clickfest, then you won't be too disappointed. It's hardly worth mentioning the revenge storyline, so I won't. Overall, a pretty good mix of Parkour (unemployed thug with a funny haircut jumping around on a roof) and screen-cracking fight sequences. The puzzles are only puzzles if you have trouble finding your way out of your own house every morning.

Game: eBoo Space Adventures. Review date 3 July 2011

Very good at what it does, however what it does tends to make me want to break things and punch the wall. That could just be me, you may find this to be the Thrust genre game for iOS devices for which you have been waiting all your life.

Game: 1-bit Ninja (One of the best games I ever played on an i-device, seriously). Review date 26 June 2011

Casual gamers should stay well away. The amount of stupid comments on the UK app store and a well-known touch-screen gaming forum, complaining about "no back button" are testament to the number of people who just can't handle this level of challenge. If you buy this game after reading the app store description, where it clearly states that there is no back button, please don't bother complaining that there is no back button. It makes you look a bit silly.

Game: Blupt! Review date 24 May 2011

I don't think the name is going to do this game any favours. Straight off the top of my head, why not Slingshot Soda Pop? Or countless other names that are better than Blupt?

Game: Crazy Coaster. Review date 6 May 2011

(I'll just lift their app store description) – "We come the newest and most exciting world evil advanture" (Yes, advanture). My left thumb is extremely painful for no apparent reason and I have to get it x-rayed. As you may have guessed, I'm having too much fun playing Order and Chaos

Online to write a proper review today. If you like this style of non-review, please let me know and I'll do a few more.

Game: Platform Hell. Review date 30 April 2011

Retro platform fans will almost certainly appreciate the single-screen, limited lives, impossible time-limit, pink & turquoise kick-in-the-nuts nightmare on offer here. Anyone not too sure might want to try the free version first.

Game: PAC 'N Jump. Review date 19 April 2011

It's interesting that one of Namco's highest rated iOS games isn't one of their arcade classics, ported to iOS devices with wonky controls, but a game specifically designed for the touch screen, albeit with characters, sounds and music from about 30 years ago. Keep it up, Namco, you've obviously stumbled onto some kind of bizarre winning formula.

Game: Scramble! Review date 7 April 2011

I used to play Scramble in a café called Ascari's. We called it "Ask Gary's" and I remember getting thrown out once but I can't remember exactly why. You may be thinking this has nothing to do with a review of an iPhone game, but I'm afraid it does. Sometimes you will hear a song playing and it will remind you, possibly subconsciously, of a place or a person, maybe a smell or a particular emotion. I get the same thing from some old videogames. Scramble is one of them. This remake is so close to the original that I get the same weird subliminal flashbacks that I get playing 'real' Scramble on MAME.

Game: Minotron 2112. Review date 5 April 2011

Overall, it's a great reminder of how videogames used to

be, but also a wake-up call for the blindly nostalgic – because they were never really quite this good.

Game: Ninja, Please! Review date 1 April 2011

I'll take all the flak and fist-waving anger from dissatisfied customers, it will be worth it. There's a lot that could be fixed in this game, but that honestly isn't the point. It doesn't matter that it says "Magic" when you buy "Health" points and I found it genuinely amusing that trying to resume a game where you had died caused it to crash. These are not huge issues. The huge issue, I fear, is that the world might not be ready for something quite this silly. And that's a sad indictment of the world, not of Ninja, Please!

Game: Sketch Ball. Review date 30 March 2011

it's a good idea but there's one slight problem. If you draw a kind of umbrella line over the target, it gets destroyed very quickly. And you can do that same thing over and over again, at least up to level 10, at which point I stopped because I wasn't really doing anything, just drawing a random line and watching the ball bounce around until it wiped the last pixel off the screen.

Game: War Pinball. Review date 25 March 2011

It doesn't really matter whether you think Chuck Norris is a Martial Arts icon or a born-again bible-bashing right-wing nutjob, back in 1984 the cult of Chuck Norris facts wouldn't emerge for another 20 years and the man himself was starting a crazy ride on the Colonel Braddock rollercoaster of B-movie gung-ho action nonsense as the star of the first Missing in Action movie. For me, the 2011 release of a virtual pinball table on Apple's i-devices, based on MIA, is simultaneously both bizarre and very intriguing. The fact that the table looks absolutely gorgeous and is phenomenally playable is a big bonus.

It's not just Chuck Norris, though. Fiancé shooting, yo-yo careered, pornstar-dating rehab veteran, Charlie Sheen has two tables in the line-up. The Platoon table is suitably challenging – presenting you with a year-long tour of duty in the 'nam, each day counting by on an animated calendar. For me, Platoon is a very close runner-up to the MIA table, but that's purely personal preference. Both of these are instant classics.

Game: Gravonaut. Review date 23 March 2011

Initially, I thought I'd have to quit after a couple of levels because it's insanely difficult right from the start. Then, of course, I got into it. Some levels took longer than others... there's no real difficulty curve, just a succession of vertical, spiky metal walls that you have to repeatedly smack your face into in order to progress. Around level 7, I started to believe that this was some kind of gaming perfection; it didn't matter that I was dying 20 or 30 times each level because the one perfect run (and each one pretty much needs to be perfect) was about as satisfying as any videogame accomplishment I've known.

Game: Air Supply - 1bit Run. Review date 12 March 2011

Imagine Nodes of Yesod being described by someone on amphetamines who has never played it themselves and has only ever heard it being discussed by Clive Sinclair and Lemmy from Motorhead... That's kind of what this game is like.

Game: Angry Caveman. Review date 6 March 2011

This was one of the worst games I ever reviewed on Arcadelife, permanently crippled and disfigured by The Curse of Game Salad (a game creation app). Here's the review...

Where to start? Appalling movement and collision detection. Lack of an undo function. Resounding significance of the overbearing use of the colour brown. Unreliable D-Pad. Horrendous linking of "lost life" to restarting a level, given how broken the movement and collision detection is. Losing all three lives resets the game and you lose ALL PROGRESS and every completed level apart from level 1 is locked again. Frustration caused by incredibly bad movement and collision detection causing levels to become unplayable. There are 13 levels, but level 5 is so broken that you will probably never complete it.

The trouble with software that allows people to easily create games is that it allows people to easily create bad games. And then flood the app store with their bumbling, untested efforts purely because it feels good to have "released a game". Trust me, I've churned out some atrocious garbage on the PC via GameMaker but at least I've had the common decency to either hide the results away in a dark place or make them available for free as a joke.

The Arcadelife website is still there (at least at the time I'm writing this), still occasionally receiving a post about Grim

Dawn hardcore mode, or a recent iOS game I've been enthusiastic enough about to share my brief, blunt, wildly biased opinions with the one or two people who ever visit it.

Chapter 15
Live another life
'I used to be an adventurer like you…'

2011 was Skyrim year. I'd been waiting for Skyrim for ages, as had countless other Elder Scrolls fans, and it was going to be even more significant for me because I was due to be unemployed yet again at the end of the year.

The details of my redundancy are tedious, and I'll only end up sounding bitter if I talk about having my job given to a bunch of people thousands of miles away in another country just because it suits British banks to give British staff the middle finger if they can use the outsourcing of British jobs to make themselves look good on the balance sheet (see, I sound bitter). So I won't mention it, because my opinion that British banks giving British jobs to third-party companies in other countries is a morally bankrupt shit-trick isn't an opinion that needs to be shared in the pages of an autobiography about video games.

Skyrim wasn't the only game released in 2011, but it was by far the most important. Before I get into it, I'll talk about some of the other PC games I played in 2011.

The trailer for Dead Island was amazing, a gory, violent, heart-rending, reverse-time sequence showing a family being savagely slaughtered by zombies in a plush holiday hotel. There was no way the game was going to live up to the expectations set by the incredible trailer, was there? No, there wasn't, and it didn't. Dead Island was an okay zombie game that degenerated into a repetitive, boring shooter with bullet-sponge super zombies and human enemies who had uncanny aim skills, and it wasn't as if PC gamers didn't already have enough repetitive boring shooters to choose from. Dead island is actually worth getting, just to play through the first part, until you reach the city. After that, I can't honestly recommend it. The trailer is still incredible, maybe one day we'll get a game that lives up to it.

Next, another game with a title where the first word is 'Dead'. It's a sequel, but I won't hold that against it because Dead Space 2 was a pretty nice game. Okay, it wasn't pretty and it wasn't nice; it gave us more of the SF gore-fest we loved in the first game, and it turned everything up a few notches just in case there were any players left who hadn't already been desensitised by the blood-splattered dismemberment overload.

Another sequel I started playing was Witcher 2, but I lost interest in it early on and never went back to it. The third game in the series is much better, although I've made similarly poor progress through that one but for different reasons, mostly related to spending the majority of my free time since 2012 writing novels instead of playing video games.

Bastion, Terraria and The Binding of Isaac all had their initial releases in 2011, three classic indie games that are popular and highly rated, although I didn't play them until a few years after they came out so I lose some gamer points there.

Of course, you didn't think I was going to forget about Minecraft, did you? It came out exactly one week after Skyrim, with graphics that looked like they came from one week after the first moon landing. I played Minecraft alone, and I played it with my son when he was very young. I never got hopelessly hooked on it, and neither did he. We tried to tame ocelots with zero success, but we did build some portals to The Nether and The End and we got killed a lot by zombie pig-men.

Now, try to imagine a drum roll, a bit of a fanfare, maybe some fireworks and a few streamers, because we've finally reached that date, 11/11/11, the day it was released: The Elder Scrolls V: Skyrim. I'm pretty sure I couldn't play it on release day, but I honestly can't remember exactly what happened. It might have been the bugs - standard Bethesda release features - or it might have been a Steam issue with the download.

I remember finding the start of the game quite tough the first time, and that's unthinkable now, eight years later, after playing dozens and dozens of characters (might be over a hundred), the initial escape from Helgen Keep no more than a casual jog, or alternatively an early opportunity to power-level stealth to 100 before venturing out into the world.

The first few characters I played were an Orc called Quentin: heavy armour and dual-wielded melee weapons, a stealthy archer: one of the most fun and potentially overpowered character types, and a stealthy illusionist who deliberately contracted vampirism because it seemed like a good idea. In eight years and more total game-time hours than I am willing to admit, I've only completed the Skyrim main quest twice, and I'm surprised I did it twice because once is really enough; more than enough for a large percentage of players if the global statistics on Steam are anything to go by.

Skyrim is one of those games, actually Skyrim is the only game I can think of, where wandering around finding random things to see and do is consistently the most amazing fun ever. It's a world I can come back to again and again, to paraphrase the Nitzer Ebb song 'I Am Undone' that was used in a Dark Souls 2 trailer, but I can't directly quote the exact lyrics here because of the copyright law regarding that sort of thing.

I've still got both the original Skyrim and Skyrim Special Edition installed within Steam, and I still occasionally go into the game to load up an old character for a nostalgic stroll around Whiterun or a quick scrap in a bandit camp, but I'm mostly burned out on Skyrim now. I haven't done everything in the game, I don't even know whether it's possible to know whether you've done everything in the game because there are so many things that can be done that aren't recorded by any of the in-game logs and statistics.

After levelling a diverse menagerie of characters and completing all the faction questlines from the base game, and the DLCs, I started messing about with a bunch of self-imposed challenges, just to see what could and could not be done if you took various Skyrim game mechanics to their logical conclusions, or their illogical conclusions in many cases.

Some of the ideas I had were partially original, others were 'inspired by' (not blatantly copied from, of course) things I'd read online or watched on YouTube. I created a Khajiit called Yuri Boykat (trust me, that name works on more than one level) and I gave him the basic restriction of never levelling up, while also trying to complete as many quests and do as much other in-game stuff as possible. The basic requirements for not levelling up (apart from just not doing anything at all) are to wear no armour (taking damage while wearing armour levels up the light or heavy armour skill) and to only use an unarmed fighting style. Using any type of weapon levels up the associated skill, but punching people (or dragons) in the face doesn't level anything up. There are other restrictions on what you can do, for example buying or selling anything levels up the speech skill, and any kind of crafting levels up a crafting skill. Cooking, for some reason, has no associated skill and can't be levelled up, so creating food for health regeneration and buffs is actually possible on a no-levelling character. I made a similar unarmed-combat character called Iron Fist. He looked like a cross between Hulk Hogan and David Coverdale (at the peak of his big-hair era) but he was allowed to level up, so he could wear some armour and make enchanted items.

Rather more fun, and requiring a lot more lateral thinking, was a character I called Zero. That one was given the challenge of not killing anything at all, ever, while still levelling up, progressing through the game, and completing as many quests as possible. Levelling up without killing wasn't any kind of a problem because all sorts of non-combat skills can easily be increased as high as you like. Completing quests was more of a puzzle. The main skill-tree I used and abused was Illusion magic.

There are Illusion spells like 'Fury' which cause the target of the spell to be treated as an enemy by any nearby NPC. Entire bandit camps could be cleared by causing fights to break out by hitting a couple of bad guys with 'Fury' and watching them start beating the crap out of each other.

The other way to eliminate enemies without the kills being recorded in your game statistics was to use the environment against them. For example, shooting an arrow at a lamp hanging above a patch of ground covered in spilled oil (you'd be surprised how careless those bandits are) will cause the lamp to fall and ignite the oil. The death of any bandit killed in the ensuing conflagration will not be attributed to the player. By combining Illusion spells with tactical use of environmental hazards, a whole bandit camp could eventually be cleared while keeping the number of kills recorded as zero.

Early on in the main quest, there's a long dungeon crawl

culminating in the first boss fight of the game, in Bleak Falls Barrow. I thought I'd get stuck at that point, but I lured the boss enemy a long way back through the dungeon to a set of pendulum traps in a narrow corridor and I used a combination of fury and calm spells to keep him running back and forth in the corridor until the traps finished him off. The only quests where it was impossible to proceed were the ones where an 'essential NPC' had to be killed, and only the player could do it. I spent ages trying to cause a Dark Brotherhood contract target to be killed by wild animals or town guards but the muppet just wouldn't die unless the player killed him.

During a few (okay, eight) years of playing Skyrim on and off, my opinion on the 'best skills' went through several changes. I used to think Stealth was the absolute best skill-tree ever, and it certainly is extremely powerful, particularly for archers and back-stabby dagger wielders, and obviously it's great for vampires and anyone remotely interested in joining the Thieves Guild. Yes, Stealth was great, and I used it on a lot of my characters, but it's not my final choice for best skill in the game.

Illusion wasn't an immediately attractive skill-tree. Initially lacking knowledge of Skyrim's Illusion spells, I dismissed it based on assumptions drawn from my experiences in previous RPG adventures. Destruction magic made sense: set things on fire, or freeze them, or zap them with lightning. Illusion sounded like pointless role-playing geek magic, and I've never been a huge fan of playing mage characters anyway; I've always preferred hitting things with big swords or sneaking about, optionally sniping with a bow. Illusion looked like a weak filler skill-tree for tree-hugging mages, but I was wrong about that, massively underestimating how overpowered Illusion magic could be, particularly for sneaky characters who had no other magic skills.

Skyrim itself heavily hinted at how good some of the Illusion spells were for stealth characters; there's a huge clue right there in the Vampire bonus to Illusion spells. At its highest level, Illusion magic can affect the undead and automatons, so, for example, you can cast Fury and Calm spells on them. And that makes you ridiculously powerful in almost every situation. The other really cool thing about Illusion is it's quick-and-easy to level up. Much easier than Destruction and arguably easier than Conjuration, which I found needed quite a lot of attribute points in magic to spam-cast bound weapons while in the presence of an enemy. Illusion can be levelled all the way up using a low-level 'Muffle' spell, you just need a bit of cash to pay for a room at an Inn so you can sleep every time you run your magic all the way down. However, despite its ease of levelling, crazy power at high level, and usefulness for otherwise non-magic characters, Illusion still didn't end up as my best skill ever in Skyrim.

For me, after hundreds of hours on way too many different characters, I finally decided the best skill in the game isn't a fighting skill, or a magic skill, or a crafting skill. It's Pickpocket. Yes, I know. I know. Really, I know. Because the only way Pickpocket is any practical use (not including pure role-playing) is if you combine it with quick-saving. And, yes, I know quick-saving is a lame way to play, purely there for noobs and losers. I know. I get it. But stay with me for a while, this will eventually make sense.

After playing lots of characters, I still wanted to play more characters but I didn't want to spend absolutely ages levelling up a particular build to find out whether it was fun or not. Enter Pickpocket. Combined with tactical save-spamming, Pickpocket can be levelled up extremely quickly, and it can be used to steal back any money you pay to a skill-trainer NPC after receiving training in any other skill. Arguably, Pickpocket plus quick-saving breaks the Skyrim experience on a fundamental level. It is also the single best shortcut in the game, not including mods and extreme glitch exploits. But, and this is the big one, if you want to go into the vanilla game and just use what's available (a basic skill and a standard save feature) you can have a great time with Pickpocket. Once you add in the use of mods, and I'm going to talk specifically about the Ordinator perk overhaul mod here, Pickpocket becomes an extremely entertaining skill-tree.

The Ordinator mod (Old Skyrim and Special Ed versions exist) completely changes every skill-tree in the game, and adds additional content associated with specific perks. For Pickpocket, you get a perk where you can reverse pickpocket a special coin onto an NPC, causing them to take more damage and critical damage when you subsequently attack them. Two additional perks at higher levels add gold to the corpse of someone killed while the coin is in their inventory, and give the player a skill similar to the 'Fury' spell, which makes the NPC holder of the coin go nuts and start randomly attacking anyone nearby. Ordinator is a fabulous mod, one I've kept enabled ever since first trying it out.

There are a couple of good mods for changing the way you play Skyrim, if you want to switch off the main quest and the dragons altogether, or if you want to play as a different character who isn't The Dragonborn. Alternate Start - Live Another Life is one, and Skyrim Unbound is the other. There are other mods that do similar things, but I found those two to be the best, although choosing one over the other is far more advisable than trying to run them both, as they tend to change some of the same parts of the game so you can end up with unexpected weirdness with both of them enabled, assuming the game doesn't just crash out when you try to start a new game.

Apart from those two or three totally game-changing mods, I never went that crazy adding gameplay mods to Skyrim. I've got a whole load of cosmetic mods to make everything look prettier or more realistic, and some mods for additional weapons and armour, but most of the other mods I tried out didn't last very long.

It's almost tempting to switch all the mods off and try playing vanilla Skyrim one more time, but only 'almost'.

My favourite guild and/or questline has to be the Dark Brotherhood. It's a bit too easy to join them, and not all the quests are as fun as they could be, but overall it's worth getting into the DB as soon as possible on any stealthy character just for the unique armour set you are given when you join. Even without glitching or extreme speed running, it's simple to get the armour on a new character within fifteen minutes of leaving Helgen Keep.

Thieves Guild is a close second place to Dark Brotherhood; if you've got the Dragonborn expansion (it's included in Special Ed) there's a fairly quick way to get an excellent full set of Blackguard's armour after completing the first few quests of the Thieves Guild questline. Mixing and matching items from that set and the Dark Brotherhood set will give you a distinct advantage in numerous situations.

The Mages Guild is okay but the quests are a bit of a slog, and Skyrim's version of the Warriors Guild is fine if you want to try playing as a werewolf, but otherwise it's just something to do once and forget about, rather like the main quest.

The Daedric artefact quests vary in terms of length, fun, and whether the item is even worth acquiring. The majority of unique Daedric artefacts are considerably weaker than the items a player can craft, once they get Enchanting or Smithing levelled up. If you're playing a no-crafting character (it is certainly viable, and a heck of a lot less grindy) you might want to concentrate on acquiring a few of the more useful Daedric artefacts. There's a very nice two-handed sword at the end of a short, easy, level-twenty quest where you don't have to go any further than Whiterun and Dragonsreach. That's always worth doing on any character, and it's mindlessly easy if you've got decent Pickpocket skills.

2012 was the year of Far Cry 3 and Diablo 3. I played a few other games, such as Dishonoured, Torchlight 2 and Angry Birds Star Wars, and I went to the gym every day. I was out of work the whole of 2012 and the first month of 2013, the longest period in my working life when I haven't had a job. I started writing novels with enthusiasm and dedication in 2012, jumping on the Fifty Shades bandwagon but starting too late to have anything ready for publication before the genre was already a totally saturated cesspit.

Far Cry 3 is a great game to play while unemployed, in fact I think that was their official tag-line in the adverts. In amongst the driving, shooting and adult content (which in Far Cry 3 meant swearing, drug abuse, boobs, and gay rape), they added a whole repetition-fest of Assassin's Creed inspired radio-tower climbing. It was awkwardly familiar, far more of a blatant copy than any kind of homage or parody. Climb each of the increasingly tricky towers, reach the top and watch the spinny in-game cut-scene while more of the map is revealed. It was exactly the same as Assassin's Creed, but that wasn't entirely a bad thing. I enjoyed climbing the towers, they were fun diversions from the main quest-line and the shooting, and they gave the same sensations of achievement and progression as they did in Assassin's Creed.

The Far Cry 3 story was compelling, but the adult content was extreme enough to feel like it had been overdone to appeal to teenagers, which made it perfect for me at forty-eight. I completed the main quest, climbed every radio tower, and completed every base takeover. Like I said, it was a great game to play while unemployed.

I didn't realise how bad Diablo 3 was until I read all the raging posts and watched all the frothing videos on YouTube. One thing I do agree with, and that is how Blizzard did completely mess up by trying to make Diablo 3 some kind of pay-to-win cash-grab, but they stopped doing that after receiving enough positive encouragement from loyal fans. Diablo 3 had hardcore mode. I avoided it for a while, which was the rational, sensible thing to do; a wise, informed choice based on the lessons I had learned while playing its predecessor. I stayed rational and sensible for about as long as it took me to play a normal, sane (non-hardcore) character three-quarters of the way through the lowest difficulty level of the game.

I created a Barbarian class character called Rollins in hardcore mode, and I promised myself I'd take it steady, avoid reckless behaviour, and get the heck out at the slightest sign of anything remotely unsafe. The level cap was sixty. The plan, as always, was to reach it without dying. At level fifty-eight, after sixty-five hours of game time, I did something reckless, stuck around too long, and got Rollins killed. I'd been posting regular updates of my Diablo 3 hardcore progress on the Arcadelife website as the Diablo 3 Hardcore Diary. The closing entry ended with the line: 'The main difference between Rollins with his one life, and me - at least he had a life.'

I was disappointed with myself for getting Rollins killed when he was so close to reaching max level, and I knew it would have been possible, even relatively easy, because the mistake that killed him was the result of overconfident carelessness rather than anything significantly tough in the game. A few minutes after Rollins got that permanent game over, I did what any rational, sensible, unemployed gamer would have done: I created a new Barbarian hardcore character called Suicidal, a female character that time because I was diverse and inclusive even back in the dark ages of 2012. Blizzard definitely were, because their female Barbarian wasn't a cute little thing; she was a big, tough mama who actually looked like she could swing a two-handed club hard enough to take your head clean off.

I didn't post any more hardcore progress updates on Arcadelife, I just concentrated on getting all the way to level sixty without dying. It ended up taking a few hours less than the failed attempt with Rollins. I published a single, celebratory post on Arcadelife including an embedded YouTube video of the Hardcore Level Sixty achievement and some hints and tips based on the skills I'd chosen, my endgame gear, and the most optimal XP farming spots for hardcore levelling. It was my first completely successful attempt at a hardcore character, and by 'successful' I mean the character reached maximum level without dying. As far as it being the type of success you could, for example, talk about down the pub, no, probably not.

2012 was the last year when I spent a large percentage of my free time playing video games. I haven't completely quit, I can't imagine I'd find it possible to completely quit, but since I started writing novels I try to find time to write rather than to play Doom (2016 version), Hitman (2016 version), Grim Dawn, Darkest Dungeon, and a bunch of other games that have caught my attention in recent years.

The latest PC games I've completed were Grim Dawn and Alien Isolation. I've been playing Grim Dawn sporadically since it was first released, my interest rekindling with each paid expansion and free content update. I've got more hardcore characters on the roster (still alive, that is) than normal-mode characters, and I reached level 100 for the first time, and beat the base game in Ultimate difficulty, on a hardcore character. I've come to terms with the inevitable loss of playing in hardcore mode, by developing a realistic perspective on life and accepting that the stuff that happens in a video game is not important enough to get upset about. Play hardcore for a proper test of your gaming skills, not because you think you're going to live forever.

I've lost enough high-level Grim Dawn characters, and all their loot, to be able to say this: it doesn't matter, and it's all part of the fun. There's a strange thrill, a rush if you like, when a hardcore character irreversibly checks out with an inventory stash full of rare gear. There's a purer thrill of relief if you hit the Esc button in time to cheat death, but sometimes you're going to be too slow, or you're just going to get one-shotted when you're not anticipating it. Live and learn. Or, more accurately, die and learn and start again.

Alien Isolation is the best Alien game ever, if we're talking about games that attempt to emulate the atmosphere and the situation of the original Alien film. The Aliens versus Predator games were mostly decent, but they were more Aliens than Alien in terms of theme and action. It's obviously much easier to make a first-person shooter with aliens and predators as the enemies than to create a survival horror style game with an unkillable Alien as the constant jump-scare threat in an environment so true to the original Alien movie that you feel like you're really there, in that time and place, even though Alien Isolation is set on a huge space station instead of the Nostromo. Well, at least until you get the DLC for the two short episodes set on the actual Nostromo.

I spent more time hiding under desks and in air vents in Alien Isolation than in any other game I've ever played. Hiding is essential. For much of the game, if you run, the alien will hear you and you're going to die. And if you operate any machinery, or shoot anything, it's going to end the same way. Alien Isolation is a hard game, and much of the time it's a viciously frustrating game. You can't kill the damn alien, the androids are complete psycho bastards and the few people you meet are too soon-to-be-dead to be any use to you, or they screw you over to save their own skins. Blame everyone who ever asked for a proper Alien game, because we got exactly what we asked for. They might have gone just a little bit over the top with the androids near the end of the game, but the rest of the experience more than makes up for it. Those damn facehuggers, though. You learn to hate them very quickly.

Darkest Dungeon has both the bleakest premise and the

most extensive and intriguing narrator dialogue of any game. It takes the generic concept of turn-based dungeon-crawling party combat, and twists the challenge into a hopeless struggle against the loss of sanity within gloomy, corrupted environments where success is no longer measured in gold but in how many party members limp home without horrendous mental illnesses. The highest level fighter still alive on your roster may have a decent sword, but he might also have kleptomania, which means he could randomly decide to take some of the valuable loot you spent an hour fighting to obtain. He might also be addicted to the tavern, or banned from the brothel, either of which could seriously affect his recuperation between missions.

The art style is straight out of the grimmest graphic novel you've ever seen, and every decision you're forced to make is only ever a choice between varying degrees of 'how bad will this turn out?', starting with the selection of desperate crazies who turn up to join your broken team of gibbering meltdowns.

It comes close to being a game that would only appeal to masochists, but fans of beautifully written, dramatically narrated dialogue won't want to miss out on the special treats to be found within the Darkest Dungeon. Fun isn't exactly the word I'm looking for, but the game is a lot of fun on PC, and also surprisingly enjoyable on an iPad due to the decent job they did translating the controls to the touch screen.

Occasionally, I had to wonder how much more fun Darkest Dungeon might be without all the raging insanity, religious zeal, brothel visits and heart attacks, but that's the whole point of the game, best summarised in the words of the narrator: "To fight the abyss, one must know it."

Chapter 16

Rave rejection
'In time, you will know the tragic extent
of my failings.'

The first full-length novel I finished writing, back in 2001, was a fantasy novel called Ravenblade. An agent showed an interest in it, and it was being considered by a publisher, but this all fell through when the contact at the publisher left their job. If I ever decide to do anything with Ravenblade it will need a considerable amount of rewriting to get it into a state where I think it's anywhere near being good enough to publish.

I rediscovered writing novels while I was unemployed in 2012, thinking I could knock out a Fifty Shades type book and become an instant millionaire. Kissing The Scorpion turned out to be a piss-take of institutionalised corporate idiocy with a few graphic-but-amusing sex scenes and a fair amount of pop-culture references. I put a lot of effort into punting it around a whole load of agents but nobody was interested. I wasn't really surprised, but it was still disappointing; my test readers said they enjoyed it, and at the time it was the best writing I could do. I honestly thought it could have had a chance at being the next big thing, in fact a published author who read it told me that, pretty much verbatim.

I found out about KDP - Kindle Direct Publishing, and I decided I'd try it because it was a legitimate method of self-publishing a book and making it available to buy on Amazon. It wasn't vanity publishing, which is essentially paying a company a lot of money to print a limited number of books that end up forgotten in your loft; there's no up-front cost involved in the Amazon KDP process, apart from the time you invest in writing the books.

I tried to get a supposedly decent cover designer to design the cover for Kissing The Scorpion, but he did a piss-poor job and I ended up paying him for his time but not using his cover. You'd think I might have learned a valuable lesson from that, but I didn't. I gave a local tattooist a deposit payment to design a tattoo for the cover of Playing The Ace, the sequel to Kissing The Scorpion, and he never did anything, never replied to any of my texts or answered any of my calls. I wish him nothing but endless bad luck and a foetid trickle of vile customers. Don't be a shithead, because one day someone will mention you in passing in their autobiography, and that's all you'll ever be worth.

Ben helped me out a lot with Kissing The Scorpion. He did the photo I've been using as my author portrait for the last seven years, and he did the cover of Kissing The Scorpion for me. While that book was sitting on Amazon, selling zero copies and remaining unnoticed (the fate of the majority of self-published novels), a friend suggested I should try writing vampire erotica.

I was halfway through writing the sequel to Kissing The Scorpion but I already knew it was going to be equally as unsuccessful, so I wrote a few chapters of a smutty vampire book called Midnight Cocktail. I liked the way it turned out enough to keep going, with a fair amount of renewed writing enthusiasm. As a few reader reviews mention, the first half of the book is mostly porn and the second half has more action and even some sort of a story. What happened, was I started out intending to just write a few chapters of filth but I got into the pulp noir style and I started to like the characters so much that I wanted to give them the story I thought they deserved. Of course, they didn't get that story until I wrote the sequel, Cheating Sunrise, which is a proper full-on thriller with the smut turned right down and the action cranked up as high as I could get it.

The two sequels to Kissing The Scorpion (Playing The Ace, Painting The Dragon) are chronological continuations of the story. I wouldn't personally describe the trilogy as "The Lord of the Rings of filthy, feel-good Bloke-Lit" but someone might, one day, possibly if I pay them enough. There might even be a 'Part Four', but it's not even on my priority list of books to write next.

With three books in an unnoticed smut series and two in the totally saturated vampire genre, I decided to try a completely new market: crime. I've read a lot of crime novels, everything from Ed McBain through James Lee Burke to Lee Child and Christa Faust. I'd previously talked myself out of writing a crime novel because I seriously doubted my ability to structure a decent plot. I did some research, found out crime plots are easier to construct if you start with the end and the twists and work backwards to the starting points. For a reader, the plot reveals are like jaw-dropping magic tricks, or at least that's how they should turn out.

My aim is to entertain, not just to write, so I set about creating my first crime thriller - Cold Inside - with that attitude, and I'm still pleased with the final outcome of all the research, plotting, and the overriding emphasis on entertaining my readers. Now all I need are some readers.

I started planning the sequel before I finished Cold Inside. I knew I wanted to write something that wasn't another serial killer thriller, and I was keen to have fun with the whodunnit concept, leaving a survivor at the scene of a massacre right at the start instead of having the usual escalating body count, although there's that too. Old Scars was my seventh published novel. I didn't even bother trying to get an agent to pick it up. My writing has improved with each book, but I'm no longer naive enough to think I'm going to have the next big bestseller, or any kind of seller.

I received what is known as a rave rejection for Cold Inside, where an agent told me everything they loved about the sample chapters, then said they wouldn't bother trying to get a publisher interested because nobody is willing to take a chance on a new crime author, no matter how good they are.

I have to assume all the traditionally published debut crime novels I see every week on Amazon and in the book section in Tesco are either written by new authors who have friends in the industry, or by established authors writing under a pseudonym.

It's hard not to feel disappointed and pissed off with this situation, even harder not to sound pissed off and bitter about it. Without blowing thousands on a marketing budget, all I can do is keep writing, and keep asking people to read my books. The writing is all down to me. As for the reading, that's up to you.

Chapter 17
Top Ten Lists
'Flawless Victory'

I spent more time going back and forth on the whole 'Shall I finish with some top ten lists?' conundrum than I spent trying to choose the chapter titles and quotes. It still seems like a not entirely brilliant idea, but it also feels like the right way to finish this book.

I'll repeat my standard disclaimer: these top ten lists are just my opinion, at the time of typing them right here, right now. They are likely to change (after this book is published), and I'm not making any claims that they're definitive lists of the best games ever.

The numeric order of each list is mostly random, but not necessarily so. If you assume I prefer the number 1 game to the number 10 game in a list, you're probably right. However, every game in a list is one I really liked, and still do.

I'll start with my top ten favourite arcade games, meaning games I played in amusement arcades, chip shops, pubs, record shops, or any other not-at-home location, mostly during the eighties.

1. Asteroids
2. Mr Do!
3. Space Invaders
4. Lunar Rescue
5. Galaga
6. Joust
7. Frogger
8. Donkey Kong
9. R-Type
10. Gauntlet

Next up, ZX Spectrum games. And I know you're going to flip back to chapter four to check whether the list here is the same as the list there. It isn't, but that should come as no surprise.

1. Manic Miner
2. The Lords of Midnight
3. Chuckie Egg
4. The Way of The Exploding Fist
5. The Hobbit
6. Bomb Jack
7. Barbarian: The Ultimate Warrior
8. Knight Lore
9. Jet Pac
10. Uridium

Between the Spectrum and the first IBM PC I owned, the

computer I played a whole lot of games on was the Atari ST. Here's my list of top ten favourite games on that machine.

1. Gunship
2. Oids
3. Dungeon Master
4. Speedball 2
5. International Karate + (IK+)
6. Midwinter
7. Return to Genesis
8. Rick Dangerous
9. Xenon 2: Megablast
10. Captain Blood

Here's my Sega Megadrive (Genesis) top ten. No, it's not deliberately controversial. If you get to number 8 and you think I just typed some random letters, I didn't; Gynoug was a cracking shoot-em-up and I'm glad I didn't miss it completely in amongst all the more-hyped Megadrive releases.

1. Flashback
2. Thunder Force IV
3. Castle of Illusion starring Mickey Mouse
4. Revenge of Shinobi
5. Strider
6. Desert Strike
7. Road Rash 2

8. Gynoug
9. Turrican II
10. Sonic The Hedgehog

Now I've done a Megadrive top ten, I have to do a Super Nintendo top ten, don't I? Here it is.

1. ActRaiser
2. Castlevania IV
3. Skyblazer
4. Contra III
5. Super Ghouls 'N Ghosts
6. Super Mario World
7. Super Mario Kart
8. Super Tennis
9. The Legend of the Mystical Ninja
10. Super Metroid

I didn't own enough NEO-GEO games to do a top ten, so I'll just do a quick PlayStation top ten before getting to the one where I know I'm going to really struggle. PlayStation top ten is easy, here we go.

1. Gran Turismo
2. Blood Omen: Legacy of Kain
3. Metal Gear Solid
4. Resident Evil
5. Tony Hawk's Pro Skater 2

6. Vandal Hearts
7. Soul Blade
8. Final Fantasy VII
9. Crash Bandicoot
10. Tenchu: Stealth Assassins

Damn, now I've got to do a PC games top ten. This is going to be set up differently from the other lists, because arguably anything decent released in the last ten years is going to look a million times better than the games we were playing in the early nineties, and the scope and content of triple-A games has dramatically changed over time. This top ten is going to be all about the effect the games had on me, at the time, and how I remember the experience of the games rather than how jaw-dropping the graphics were, or not. No more procrastination, here's my top ten most fondly remembered PC games of all time ever, at the time of writing.

1. Doom
2. Crusader: No Remorse
3. Skyrim
4. Deus Ex
5. Half-Life 2
6. Baldur's Gate 2
7. Diablo 2
8. Tomb Raider
9. Thief: The Dark Project
10. Unreal Tournament

That's it. If I came back after thinking about the list for another hour, half of those might be different. It's not worth adding a list of 'almost made the list' games because there are dozens, and they're all great for their own reasons.

One hour later...

Can't believe I missed Fallout 2 off that list! It should be in the top five. See, that's what happens when I come back and read through the list an hour later. And where the heck is Grim Dawn? Not on my original list, that's for sure. Sorry, Crate Entertainment, I honestly love that game.

There you have it, a meandering journey through a life of video games, inextricably tangled up with real-world adventures.

I haven't been left gibbering and mentally scarred by video games, but I also can't imagine how my life might have turned out if they hadn't been part of it. At the very least, I wouldn't have spent a few hundred enjoyable hours on this book. I started writing this on the seventh of March, 2014. It kept getting shelved due to the novels I've been writing, but halfway through 2019 I decided to rewrite what was already there, and get the damn thing finished. If you made it this far, there's a fair chance you were entertained, and that's what it's all about.

AUTHOR'S NOTE

Thank you for reading Arcade Life - Live versus Video Games.

Please can you take a few minutes to leave a review of this book on Amazon. As an independent author I really appreciate reader feedback, and I also rely on it to provide invaluable assistance spreading the word about my books.

To discover more of my books, a great place to start is my author page on Amazon:

http://www.amazon.co.uk/J.W.-Tapper/e/B00Q5IGOZQ

That is the '.co.uk' version, but your region should have a similar page.

If you would like to find out some more about me, my writing, and my other interests, I have a blog and details of current and forthcoming books on my website: http://jwtapper.co.uk

The other book series I've published are:

The Truth About Kate Hayes

Currently a trilogy, with the fourth instalment 'done when it's done', this is a bloke-lit contemporary romance series following the risqué escapades of Dave Fletcher and the seductive, mysterious, and frequently downright filthy Kate Hayes.

Books in this series are 'Kissing The Scorpion', 'Playing The Ace', and 'Painting The Dragon'.

Blood:Lust

This series of neo-noir vampire novels currently includes 'Midnight Cocktail' and 'Cheating Sunrise'.

Humberside CID

This series of crime novels is set during the 1980s in England, UK, mostly in and around Kingston upon Hull. The first book in the series is 'Cold Inside'. 'Old Scars' is the chronological sequel, but the books do not have to be read in order, although you can expect a certain degree of spoiler content if you read the second one first.

Samples of all my books are available via Amazon's 'Look Inside' feature for both paperback and Kindle versions.

J.W. Tapper - March 2020

Printed in Great Britain
by Amazon